D1607394

Tales of a Great Lakes Sailor

The Evolution of a Landlubber

by

William E. Cornell, Jr.

INFINITY
PUBLISHING

Copyright © 2010 by William E. Cornell, Jr.

ISBN 0-7414-5833-0

Printed in the United States of America

Published March 2010

INFINITY PUBLISHING
1094 New DeHaven Street, Suite 100
West Conshohocken, PA 19428-2713
Toll-free (877) BUY BOOK
Local Phone (610) 941-9999
Fax (610) 941-9959
Info@buybooksontheweb.com
www.buybooksontheweb.com

To Carol for putting up with it all.

Contents

Introduction

This narrative tells how and why a person begins and subsequently continues to enjoy the pleasures and sometimes terrifying experiences of sailing over a forty-year period, specifically the Great Lakes for thirty-five of those forty years. Included are not only some of the elements of sailing, but also some of the on shore experiences, limited descriptions of places, and some of the characters encountered.

While the fuel necessary to produce the fiberglass and synthetic materials detracts from the green earth environment, sailing complements some of today's increasing green environment values in that comparatively little fuel is consumed. The yachtsman is restrained by not only government regulation, but also a personal conscientiousness to attempt to keep the water environment pristine. Consider the controls instituted to keep oil, garbage, sewage, and industrial waste from our water system. Most boaters eagerly accept and help to enforce these regulations. Who wants a dirty and contaminated playground?

The decline of industry around the Great Lakes evolving into the "rust belt" has partially resulted in the improvement of the Great Lakes environment, especially Lake Erie. This also, as observed from the deck of a small sailboat, has resulted in a substantial decrease in shipping during the last forty years.

Meeting the challenges of traveling by using wind power, surviving variable weather conditions, navigating courses, entering unknown waters and harbors and learning the regulations required for the safe operation of a vessel, if properly applied, can be rewarding experiences.

This book was not written as a how to do it exercise, but certain explanations and notes are included only to give an understanding of some items and concepts, which are referred to and may not be familiar to the reader. In addition to keeping the author entertained, this was written for armchair adventurers and wanna-be sailors. Perhaps even other sailors and power boaters, experienced and inexperienced, might derive some enjoyment.

Some of the names have been changed not only to protect the innocent, but also to protect the author. Any similarity to persons living or dead is purely intentional.

Growing Up With Lake Erie

Lake Erie has been a part of my life since I was a baby. I vaguely remember at about the age of four my cousin Art and I were questioning whether the lake at Euclid Beach Park was the same lake we saw near our Grandmother's house several miles away. We slowly came to the realization that it was. Wow! How could anything be so big?

During the last years of World War II occasional trips were made to the beach where my job was to fill my little pail with sand using the accompanying little shovel supplied by my mother.

As I grew older, my parents always seemed to rent a house or apartment relatively near the lakeshore. Accessibility to the lake was always available. It was during this time, the late 1940's and early 1950's, that my friends and I would seek adventure along the lake shore, first at a beach on the east side of Cleveland. This area was called White City Beach. The White City Beach area had a roadway, which ran from Lake Shore Blvd. down to the water. Between the water and Lake Shore Blvd. was a fairly extensive area of small sand dunes and scrubby vegetation, perfect for small boys to dig holes and build redoubts.

A stone break-wall extended from the shore out into the lake and formed a small-protected beach. When we tired of digging in the sand, we would hike out on the wall and look for ways to crawl between the large box-shaped stones. One day we found a way to squeeze into the cavernous opening that ran inside the wall. This was a perfect hideout for us. That is, until Lake Erie kicked up and the cracks between the stones filled with water pouring in. Time to get out of our not so perfect hideout. This experience so terrified us that wisely we decided to never again tackle the innards of the White City break-wall.

My father decided that it was time we go fishing on Lake Erie. At night, when we drove along Lake Shore Blvd. hundreds of lights could be seen out in the lake. At this time fishing from a small boat with a gasoline lantern hanging over the side was popular. My father decided that we too should experience the joy of night fishing. At first, he would rent about a fourteen-foot rowboat with an outboard motor from one of the liveries along the lakefront. Since it cost more to rent a boat with a motor, Dad shortly acquired his own Scott-Atwater outboard, which he carried in the trunk of our Studebaker.

Countless nights we'd buy night crawlers and minnows, rent a small boat, hook up the Scott-Atwater and make our way into the darkness, punctuated with the lights of hundreds of other like-minded fisherman. To this very day I marvel at how my Dad had the nerve to take a ten-year old boy in a small open boat into the unpredictability of Lake Erie. Perhaps it was the security felt from the presence of the other fisherman.

At the same time, and unbeknownst to me, Lake Erie was becoming the world's largest cesspool. Within a few years the once beautiful beaches were lined with human excrement, condoms, and dead fish. The dead fish were not only the result of raw human and industrial waste being dumped into the lake, but also the lamprey eel. Lampreys were found in Lake Ontario and the St. Lawrence River since these were connected to the Atlantic Ocean. They made their way to the other Great Lakes by way of the Welland Canal. During the 1950s dead fish lined the shore since lampreys are an aggressive blood-sucking parasite and attach themselves to fish until the fish dies. Fortunately, in 1958 scientists were able to find a chemical

4

that kills lamprey larvae and lamprey eels were, for the most part, eliminated as a problem.

About this time, it was slowly beginning to be realized that something had to be done. Industrial and human waste could not be continuously dumped into the lake. I remember riding along Lake Shore Blvd. In front of an electrical power plant at East 72nd Street a stone wall projects into the lake. Written by some local graffito practitioner, in large white letters on this wall, were the words "SAVE ME- I'M DYING-Lake Erie".

Pollution and dead fish were not to keep us from enjoying the waters of Lake Erie. We managed to find a floating raft-like object on the beach. To get away from the crud along the shore, four of us would paddle three or four miles off shore in order to go swimming. After a while we'd turn the crude vessel over and play "king of the mountain".

If we were unable to swim, because of the pollution, another activity was substituted. During and after World War II, because of heavy snowfalls in the Great Lakes watershed, the lake level had substantially increased. While this permitted the ore carriers to carry increased tonnage, the increased level played havoc with the shoreline. What had been reasonably broad beaches now disappeared as waves eroded the bluffs overlooking the lake. As a consequence, several homes and summer cottages began to gradually slip over the bluff edge and into the lake. This provided an entertaining, if dangerous playground. We joyfully crawled around in these tilted structures, oblivious of the fact that they may tumble over the edge at any minute. We were lucky.

Wintertime did not dampen our enthusiasm for exploration. Now, we were not limited to the shoreline. We could hike out over the frozen surface pretending we were Arctic explorers. Because of shifting ice and the build-up of ice ridges and crevasses, everyday was a new exploration adventure. Fortunately, we were again lucky not to fall into a crevasse or pursue our Arctic like adventure when the ice flows broke away from the shore.

Of course, we never let our parents know some of the foolish things we did. They were already scared to death of polio possibly a result of swimming in Lake Erie. 1952 was the height of the polio scare when over 60,000 cases were reported. No one really knew if swimming in the lake caused polio, but many parents thought so. Because of the pollution, this seemed to be a logical assumption.

By the early the 1950s, my father had become an avid fisherman. He would take my younger brother and me to Fairport Harbor about thirty miles northeast of Cleveland. Here we could fish off the shored up banks of the Grand River and watch the ore boats and pleasure craft make their way up and down the river. In between trips to a local restaurant, "Evans Lunch", for sodas and snacks, we'd catch perch, white bass and an occasional catfish, which were the most fun. There were still some commercial fishing boats, but these were to be gone from U.S. waters within a few years as pollution continued to take its toll.

Upon occasion my family, including grandparents, would rent a cabin for a week of fishing at Kelly's Island. Kelly's Island is located toward the less polluted southwest portion of Lake Erie. The most exciting thing about going to Kelly's Island was the ride by ferry from the mainland. The next most exciting thing for a kid was the glacial grooves. About as exciting as watching a tire with a slow leak go flat. What kids have to go through to please their parents.

In 1956, my parents finally took me away from the lake when they moved inland to Twinsburg, Ohio, some twenty-five miles south of Lake Erie. This move along with time at Kent State University and jobs in Akron, Ohio kept Lake Erie from having a further impact on me. That is, except for occasional trips to Cleveland where I could spot larger commercial vessels out upon the lake.

6

One of these was the Aquarama. This was an aquamarine colored passenger vessel, which carried passengers and automobiles between Cleveland and Detroit. Originally a troop carrier for service to Europe during the last days of World War II, the converted Aquarama was the largest passenger ship ever utilized on the Great Lakes. Unfortunately, the unprofitable Aquarama discontinued service in 1962. During the 1980's on one of the several sailing trips to northern waters, I again spotted the now derelict vessel docked on the Canadian side of the upper section of the St. Clair River. I understand she was later sold for scrap. As is too often the case, an inglorious end to a beautiful vessel.

Numerous cargo ships were often seen off shore. These appeared somewhat mysterious when viewed from afar. Little did I know that someday the ore carriers would not be so distant. In the early 1960s, during summers off from Kent State, I worked as a firemen on the New York Central Railroad. I usually worked out of what was known as Collinwood Yard located on the east side of Cleveland.

Rail jobs in Cleveland were cut because of a steel workers strike, affecting those railroaders with the least seniority. In order to work, I had to take up residence in a boarding house in Ashtabula where railroad jobs were available. One of the railroad jobs was to work in the harbor positioning gondola cars along a wharf so they could be loaded by Hulett unloaders with iron ore from Great Lakes freighters. When the cars were positioned, the engineer and I had to wait until the cars were loaded before bringing another set of cars along the ore freighter. This gave us the opportunity to go aboard the freighter and have a snack with some of the crew. After years of viewing these monoliths from afar, I was now close enough to truly appreciate their size.

Well into the 1960s, pollution continued to be a concern. I remember reading in one of the weekly news magazines that only a forty-mile square area of Lake Erie was still capable sustaining life. In 1969, Cleveland achieved infamous notoriety when the Cuyahoga River caught fire. The river had caught fire several times previously, but this fire was given national attention when mentioned in a weekly news magazine. Cleveland became the object of late night television jokes. The important thing was that this fire brought national attention to poor environmental conditions not only for the Cuyahoga River, but also, throughout the country.

Eventually my attention to Lake Erie returned when I began sailing on the lake in 1974. Initially, I was pleasantly surprised at how much improvement had been made with regard to pollution on the lake. Beds of a green plant like substance were found in the water, but these began to disappear within a few years.

In 1980, I secured a position with the Sherwin-Williams paint company. My office overlooked the Cuyahoga River and specifically what was known as Collision Bend. Here, I could watch the ore boats assisted by tug boats make the tight turns in the river on the way up to and down from the steel mills up river. No longer did the river catch fire.

Lake Erie's latest condition centers with the zebra mussel. These tiny fingernail size creatures originated in the Caspian Sea and somehow were able to expand into the world's oceans, the St Lawrence River and Lake Ontario. They were introduced into Lake St. Clair in the late 1980s from vessels dumping ballast and have spread to the other Great Lakes. At first there was considerable panic among boaters who thought these little creatures would foul cooling systems. While they may be costly impediments to drinking and power plant water sources, they appeared to have not disadvantaged boaters and, I'm told, actually are responsible for partially cleaning and purifying the water

Bigger is Better

It seems that many sailors, and particularly this sailor, are always looking for increasing challenges to their sailing ability. Initially this begins with increasing the size of their vessel. My first sailing experience came when my Father acquired a small nine-foot cat rigged[*] craft in 1969. My parents had a home on a small lake (Lake Latonka) in Pennsylvania and my Father acquired this little cat-rigged boat to play with when we visited.

I spent hours trying to make this little vessel do my bidding, to no avail. I read several sailing instruction books looking for the elusive secret. I knew what tacking[**] was. Still the little boat would not follow my instruction. It seemed the little thing had a mind of its own. Then one day I repositioned myself and moved from the stern to the center. Eureka. I found the secret. The little boat could now be controlled, despite the fact that I now had to man the tiller behind me. Apparently, when I sat in the stern, the boat was small enough that the bow lifted to the point where it caught the wind, making the little boat uncontrollable.

One day on my commute from work in Akron I began to think that I needed to find some sort of hobby/activity. When I entered home I announced to my wife Carol, "You know, I've been thinking I need to have some kind of extra-curricular activity." Carol then asked, "What kind of activity?" I responded, "Well, I was thinking about motorcycles or sailing." "Oh, I think I would prefer you

---

[*] Cat rig-Rig refers to the configuration of sails on a boat. A boat with a single mast and a single mainsail is said to be cat rigged.

[**] Tacking is zig-zagging in order to make headway into the wind.

take up sailing," Carol said. "Why's that?" Carol looked at me and said in all seriousness, "Well, I think it's much more romantic to say my husband was lost at sea rather than my husband was spattered against a wall in a motorcycle accident." We laughed and I said, "Sure makes a lot of sense to me."

Now that I had her blessing, my father-in-law was anxious to get into the act. He had sailed as a young man and seeing my growing interest in sailing, decided that we should do some sailing. A couple of times we rented small boats including what are called a Lightning and a Hobie Cat on inland lakes. Fortunately, he derived as much pleasure in showing me some elements of sailing as I received in being shown.

My interest was now to the point where it was time to acquire my own boat. I decided that I wanted a sloop-rigged*vessel. My flawed reasoning behind wanting a sloop-rigged vessel was that sloop-rigged vessels came in larger sizes. If I were to really get into sailing, I wanted to know how to handle a sloop.

Perusing want ads, I found a fourteen-foot homemade kit boat, (a Luger-Zephyr built by others) which was sloop rigged. This boat I christened *Escape*. It was much like a Sunfish in that the occupant sat on the edge of the deck with legs positioned in a

Escape at Lake Latonka, Pennsylvania

well. Initially, the *Escape* was transported on a car top. However, a friend Bruce Washington supplied a small trailer and the *Escape* was happily transported to and sailed on Lake Latonka all summer and into the fall of 1971.

---

* Sloop rig-refers to a configuration of sails. A boat with a single mast, single mainsail and a foresail can be said to be a sloop.

Two important lessons were learned when sailing the *Escape*. One day I lost a pair of glasses when I was pitched into Lake Latonka after the *Escape* capsized. Lesson one: wear a strap on glasses if there is a possibility of capsizing. Lesson two: release the sheet* when a strong gust of wind comes along. These small lessons more than compensated for the increasing pleasure found in sailing. For example, I remember sailing the *Escape* on Thanksgiving day marveling at the mild weather so late in the fall. Finally. I thought if Albert Einstein could learn to sail a day sailor then so could I.

Now it was time to graduate to a larger inland lake. I chose Mosquito Creek Reservoir since it was only thirty-five miles west of my home in Twinsburg. The following year I decided I wanted a

Escape II at Mosquito Creek Resevoir

larger boat with a cabin and the ability to cook aboard. I acquired a twenty-three-foot trailerable boat (Aquarius) suitable for small inland lakes. I named this vessel the *Escape II*. This was the first boat that I was able to sleep aboard and was equipped with an alcohol stove and a head (porta-pottie) despite being cramped with no head room.

As with most things, the more complicated, the more problems. Each time the *Escape II* was utilized, in addition to launching, the mast had to be stepped and rigged with stays and shrouds. One weekend while taking some friends sailing on Mosquito Creek Reservoir, the hinged

---

*Sheet-Many non-sailors think a sheet is a sail. In reality, a sheet is a line attached to and used to control a sail. If you ever heard the expression for an inebriated person, "three sheets to the wind" you now know it means out of control.

centerboard dropped and the stopper broke. Despite several hours attempting to repair, the board could not be raised. The board was finally secured by wrapping a line under the hull and pulling the board into its well. So much for sailing that day. Fortunately, my friend Bruce was able to repair the board by drilling and tapping the board and placing a repair plate on the top of the board.

The trailer for the *Escape II* had two wheels. One Sunday after returning from sailing on Mosquito Creek Reservoir one of the trailer tires went flat. Because it was Sunday, no place was open that could or would repair a flat tire. Bruce, who had become my regular crew suggested that we try to use the spare tire in my 1972 Ford. The spare fit perfectly and we were soon merrily on our way. What luck!

You should'nt have to worry about tires when you own a boat.

A Virgin Experience

I was now looking for yet another sailing challenge. I noted an ad for bare-boat chartering in the British Virgin Islands. They advertised that if you took their sailing course by mail concluding with a two day cruise in New York harbor under the auspices of one of their selected sailing captains, you would be qualified to charter one of their boats in the British Virgins. Not knowing exactly what I was getting into I signed up and began their correspondence sailing course. I studied with enthusiasm the materials including the Admiralty charts of the British Virgins.

Finally, my wife Carol and I were off to City Island located east of the Bronx in Long Island Sound for a two day training cruise in the New York harbor area, specifically Long Island Sound. City Island is a small narrow island in Long Island Sound connected to the Bronx mainland by a causeway road. The road continues down the center of the island with boat yards and sail lofts along both sides of the roadway. There we met our instructor-captain whose name was something like Deutschman. We spent two days aboard Captain Deutschman's, boat a 28-foot Pearson moored just offshore. We were instructed in the art of anchoring, boat handling, sail handling, line handling, rules of the road and numerous small details associated with Captain Deutschman's boat. Our first day of sailing was a Sunday. Long Island Sound was so crowded with vessels that it seemed you could almost cross the Sound by jumping from boat to boat.

That Sunday evening Captain Deutschman took a launch back to shore while Carol and I were to spend our first evening aboard a moored vessel. The next day Captain

Deutschman returned to the boat and again we continued our sailing experience under the auspices of Captain Deutschman. On Monday, except for a few tugs and workboats, the Sound was almost deserted. As we sailed, we continued to add to our store of sailing lingo before returning to Ohio.

Monday evening we departed for home confident in our newly acquired knowledge of sailing and prepared to take on whatever the Caribbean could dish out. We were now supposedly qualified to embark on our bare boat charter in the British Virgin Islands.

With Carol, my brother Fred, and his wife Dorothy we flew to San Juan, Puerto Rico where we were met by a local pilot for the flight to the B.V.I. "Hi! I almost forgot you guys. I was at a party this afternoon," the pilot said with the hint of an alcohol breath. As we boarded the plane (an older Beechcraft) the pilot said, "One of you will have to sit up front in the co-pilot's seat." Being the instigator of this group, I jumped at the chance. Shortly after take off I asked the pilot, "Been flying long?" "Yeh, ever since I was a B-25 pilot in WW II. With that bit of information, I began to relax and enjoy the flight. Shortly thereafter, I could see the Virgins before us. Happily, I began to recognize several of the islands thanks to my intense study of the British Admiralty Charts.

Our trip to the small hotel was a nightmare. As is customary, in a British possession, vehicles drive in the left lane. When the driver approached an on coming car head on, at the last minute, swerved to the left as we all breathed a sigh of relief. I think the driver got a real kick out of watching what he knew would be our reaction as he drove on, now with a slight smile.

When we got to our hotel we relaxed until dinner in the modestly furnished and unpretentious assigned rooms. The evening dinner was served on an open-air veranda with the ever present breeze blowing through. All was quiet except for occasional conversation and the ticking of an old grandfather clock. I noted the clock didn't show the right time. In fact, it was a few hours off. Nobody cared since this seemed to confirm and set the tone of the environment.

The next morning we were introduced to our boat, a thirty-four foot Carib (basically a Bristol 34 redesigned for cruising) named. *La Suisse* docked at Maya Cove on the main island of Tortola.

La Suisse — A 34' Bristol modified for cruising.

Before turning *La Suisse* over to us, my brother and I were taken to a brief orientation while our wives, in a typical chauvinistic fashion, were taken to La Suisse to pack food supplies. They told us not to be overly concerned about barracudas and sharks with the exception of swimming at night when the sand sharks came closer to shore to eat. We were also told we could sail into the U.S. Virgin Island area, but were encouraged to stay in the British area. It was implied that it was much safer in the British Virgins.

I would soon learn that one of the best things I had on board was "The 1971 Yachtsman's Guide to the Virgin Islands" John R. Van Ost, Editor. This book was filled with information about each of the islands and, most importantly, details about approaching anchorages, the locations of reefs, and dangerous submerged rocks.

We boarded and were off into The Sir Francis Drake Channel. I must admit that initially I was somewhat secretly terrified. I climbed on the cabin top to raise sail. I couldn't expose my initial trepidation to my novice crew. The swells were more significant than I thought they would be. After all, I had never been exposed to anything other than small inland lakes and the relative calm and protected confines of Long Island Sound. After the mainsail was raised and filled with the constant 15 to 17 knot wind, *La Suisse* settled down and began to slice through the water as she was designed to do.

We sailed across The Sir Francis Drake Channel to our first anchorage at a place called Dead Man's Bay on Peter Island. This was the first time I had sailed a deep draft boat and anchored on my own. One of the nice things about anchoring in the Virgins, you could swim out over the anchor and look through unbelievably clear, pristine water to see that the anchor was properly digging in. Overcoming the tension that came from a first time experience, I was content with relaxing at the first anchorage, cooking our first meal and consuming accompanying liquid refreshers. I had no desire to explore. Although we were safe and secure, an inner alarm clock then, as in the future, would cause me to awaken intermittently when anchoring to check and make sure the anchor was holding. To my relief it was.

The next day we took a comparatively short sail to a nearby anchorage called the Bight on Norman Island. More confident of my anchoring ability, I was now ready to explore the island. We took the dinghy ashore crossed over the small island and found some refuse, which appeared to have washed up from overseas. We then took the dinghy (rowing so as to not damage the dinghy outboard prop) into a cave opening.

Not surprising, there are a number of stories about pirates in the Virgin Island area. It is easy to imagine pirates utilizing these caves to hide their loot. Unfortunately, we, as with numerous visitors to these caves, did not come across any pirate loot.

From inside a cave while in the dinghy

The first two islands Peter and Norman were uninhabited. Just right for this first time short ventures. Unbeknownst to me at the time Caribbean Sailing Yachts had a fairly powerful telescope at Maya Cove to watch departing vessels as they initially ventured into The Sir Francis Drake Channel. This was to make sure the charter patrons were competent. In case of problems, they could relieve/rescue and terminate the charter or require the assignment of a captain. I guess I had passed the test under their watchful eye.

By now my confidence was growing. I had successfully piloted and sailed to two locations and successfully anchored twice. Wow! Maybe I am getting to be an unadulterated sailor.

The next day we departed for a longer sail around the southwest end of Tortola, the main island of the British Virgins. We passed through an area called the Narrows. The Narrows separates the island of Tortola of the British Virgin Islands from the island of St. John of the U.S. Virgin Islands. My objective was an anchorage called Cane Garden Bay on the northwest side of Tortola. Most of the bareboat chartering in the Virgins is done in the winter. Since it was July, there were not a lot of boats in the area.

We were told that in the winter boats often avoided Cane Garden Bay because of a rolling anchorage.

Cane Garden Bay coincided with our now laid back dispositions. There were no commercial stores, few, if any, vehicles except for some small flat-bed trucks, and no night life. The few inhabitants were quiet, friendly and monetarily poor. Their wealth seemed to be derived from the peacefully quiet and beautiful surroundings.

I wasn't sure of the main economic activity except harvesting some sugar cane and fruit; and fishing from the locally constructed small boats. We came to thoroughly enjoy Cane Garden Bay and its inhabitants. A Mr. Theodore Skeats, a local school master took us into one of the sugar cane fields and cut some cane for us to sample; a little girl offered us some limes, for a small tip of course. The pace of life in Cane Garden Bay was comfortably slow.

We had heard that there was a rum distillery nearby. Fred and I found, what we were told, was supposedly the oldest continuously operating rum distillery in the new world.

Mr. Theodore Skeats

As we walked in, the owner/worker was filling a bottle for an older woman. As she left, the worker turned to us. "We'd like to get some rum," I said. "Where's yu bottles?" came the response. "We don't have bottles." With that the worker disappeared into an adjacent dark room and came back with two bottles. He proceeded to wash them out with a wire brush and fill them with clear-colored rum from the faucet on a drum container. Not the quintessence of

cleanliness, but we were sure the strength of alcohol would negate any germs.

When he handed the bottles to us I asked, "Do you have any labels for the bottles?" He reached over to a slot in the wall and pulled out two labels, licked the backsides and smacked them on to the bottles. The minor cost of the product was worth it just to observe the operation and bottling of this, the supposedly the oldest continuously operating rum distillery in the new world.

Our next adventure came when we found there was transportation over the mountain to Road Town, the British Virgin capital on the south side of Tortola. We elected to take this journey on the back of a flatbed truck with benches bolted to the flat-bed. The Virgins are comprised of mountain tops rising from the bed of the ocean. The road over the mountain was narrow without guard-rails for protection against going over the side. As we continued along, abandoned cars could occasionally be seen having gone over the series of precipitous cliffs.

We didn't spend a lot of time in Road Town. After all, we were here to sail. On the way back to Cane Garden Bay the jitney occasionally picked up local passengers. One lady climbed onto the flatbed holding a small bottle of gasoline. At the time we all were smokers. Hitting a bump in the road her small, uncapped bottle fell to the flatbed floor and spread gasoline over the flatbed. Fortunately,

Cane Garden Bay

none of us were smoking at the time as we scrambled off the jitney until the spillage was cleaned. Having now arrived back at Cane Garden Bay, I decided to depart the next morning and as they say in the movies "sail with the tide." Oh yes, by the way, the tide in the Virgins is barely noticeable.

The crew unfurling the main sail.

That evening I was tending the stainless grill attached to a stanchion and hanging out from the stern over the water. Out the corner of my eye I thought I saw a grayish white something swim by. I looked over the side, but could see nothing in the water. A short time later, again I thought I saw a quick grayish white something swim by. Now, I was intent of looking over the side and sure enough there were some sand sharks. "Hey Fred, come up here and bring that old hamburger." We tossed a small ball of the hamburger over the side and watched to see what the sharks would do.

The sharks warily circled the hamburger ball, but wouldn't take it. We decided they probably didn't like hamburger or were wary of us. We finally gave up and I tossed about a three-inch hamburger ball into the darkness away from *La Suisse*. No sooner did it hit the water and we heard a brief thrashing in the water. Guess they were wary of humans. Who can blame them?

By now the crew, as well as the captain, were in pretty good shape. I had been fortunate in hiding my early anxiety from the crew and all seemed at ease. Being anxious to participate in the sailing adventure, they followed my every command relative to what to do aboard, my decisions on where to go, how to get there, how long to stay and when to depart. I guess you could say they were at my mercy. Good thing I wasn't a Captain Bligh, although they might have disagreed. In any event, captain and crew were working well together. We all appeared to act admirably as we were ready to depart Cane Garden Bay in the morning.

The next day we sailed to a place called Marina Cay an anchorage just west and near an island called Great Camanoe. The area was deserted. We went ashore, climbed up to a small pavilion with a stocked bar and a small sign which, in effect said "Help yourself. Leave money in the small box on the bar." Wow! Talk about an honor system, which we did honor.

The following day we were off to Gorda Sound a well-protected area surrounded by the island of Virgin Gorda and Prickly Pear Island. I had been warned, I'm not sure by whom, possibly during the initial orientation session, not to enter the sound from the north after 3:30 p.m. The reefs are not as visible after this time due to the sun's reflection. When we passed the initial entry bordered by reefs, the sound opened to safe deep water.

We anchored off a small area called The Bitter End. Again, the area was deserted except for a woman in charge of the place. She was exceptionally friendly due to the name of our boat *La Suisse*. She was from Switzerland. We spent two evenings frolicking, swimming and relaxing in Gorda Sound before returning to our point of origin, Maya Cove. Unfortunately, all good things must come to an end.

The final duty aboard La Suisse

On the sail back to Maya Cove we cleaned up *La Suisse* and scrubbed the deck. *La Suisse* was to be delivered in ship-shape. All pitched in as we scrubbed the deck, straightened below, washed the dishes, packed our gear and clothing, straightened the charts and cruising guide before putting in at Maya Cove.

We happily had cruised the B.V.I. for one week with out incident perhaps, due to my over riding philosophy, "Error on the side of caution." When we finally docked at Maya Cove, *La Suisse* was in ship-shape. We went through a short debriefing session. I noted, across the charter's poop sheet on me, was scribbled in large letters "WATCHOUT." Guess I showed them.

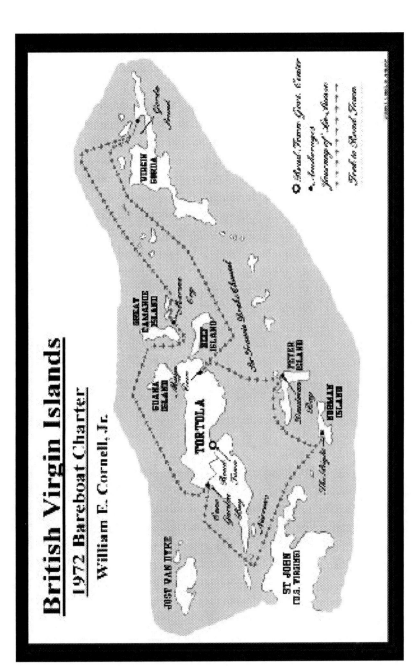

British Virgin Islands

1972 Bareboat Charter

William E. Cornell, Jr.

The Last Escape

After successfully cruising the British Virgin Islands with the perfect weather conditions of sun and constant 15 to 17 knot winds, I felt that now it was time to acquire a vessel which could handle Lake Erie.

The Dangerous Great Lakes

People who live away from and most who live near the Great Lakes are totally oblivious of the lakes as major and potentially dangerous bodies of water. Probably this is because they are comprised of fresh water and are called lakes rather than inland seas. I remember one time when I took a California business associate to socialize at my yacht club. When we entered the yacht club, upon viewing Lake Erie his mouth dropped and he said he had to call his wife in California. I thought maybe he had left a coffee pot on the burner or some other miner emergency. No, his conversation with his wife went as follows, "Vickie, you should see it. (Lake Erie) It's like an ocean. You can't see the other side." A typical reaction to a first viewing the Great Lakes.

A well known under estimate of the Great Lakes occurred in the 1960s or 1970s, when Ted Turner made derogatory comments about the Chicago to Mackinac sail race implying that the race did not offer a significant challenge compared to ocean racing. At the end of what was to become a stormy race, Mr. Turner retracted his statement and gained substantial respect for these inland seas.

Even in comparatively recent times the lakes still take their toll despite modern weather forecasts and greatly improved navigation and safety equipment. One of most startling events demonstrating the dangerous Great Lakes was that of the wreck of the Edmund Fitzgerald memorialized by the singer Gordon Lightfoot. The Edmund Fitzgerald was a modern well-equipped ore freighter that went down in Lake Superior "when the winds of November come early" as sung by Lightfoot.

In terms of size the Great Lakes are less impressive than the world's oceans. Great Lakes sizes range from Lake Ontario, a little over 7,500 square miles, to Lake Superior, over four times as large at over 31,500 square miles. This is one of the characteristics that make the lakes so dangerous since a vessel is seldom more than 40 or 50 miles from a lee shore. On the ocean where a lee shore might be 300 or 1600 miles, in bad weather, one can go below, batten down the hatches and catch forty winks. Also, traffic on the Great Lakes, as mentioned above, is considerably more intense thus, requiring a fairly constant lookout.

Other dangerous conditions include an extremely rapid change of the weather and a 10,000 square mile body of water with an exceptionally shallow depth. The deepest point in Lake Erie is 210 feet found off of Long Point, Ontario just north of Erie, Pennsylvania.

A rapid change in weather is characteristic throughout the mid-west, and consequently, on all of the Great Lakes. In the early 1970's the Cleveland area was struck with a damaging, violent storm that developed so quickly that the Weather Bureau was caught off guard and unable to give adequate warning. The result was severe damage and the consequent sinking of a number of small boats.

The shallow depth of Lake Erie is a potentially dangerous situation because waves form in a vertically cyclonic manner. In deep water, waves on the surface are generally what can be described as rolling. However, the cyclonic pattern of waves formed in shallow water is disturbed by the shallow bottom and come to the surface as breaking waves.

With the combination of rapidly changing weather and a shallow depth, Lake Erie has the reputation of being a "choppy" and consequently, a dangerous body of water.

A multitude of books have been written about the numerous vessels lost on the Great Lakes. Many of these vessels were sailing in what can be described as chancy weather (November-December) to get the last trip of the season before the lakes froze over. Never the less, the uncertainties of weather can also occur during the milder seasons.

The first sailing vessel on the Great Lakes, the *Griffin* constructed by the French explorer La Salle in 1679, suffered an inglorious end. The Griffin was built and sailed from eastern end of Lake Erie to Lake Michigan where it was lost in a storm. The modern sailor is amazed at the fact that the *Griffin* traveled so far considering that there were no charts. Getting up bound on what were to become the Detroit and St. Clair Rivers, especially where Lake Huron empties into the St. Clair river, must have been a monumental task. Men pulling tow lines along the shore must have been the rule rather than the exception with a slight respite as the Griffin made its way around the edge of or perhaps sailed across Lake St. Clair.

Sadly, after successfully overcoming these obstacles, the *Griffin* met its end somewhere on Lake Michigan becoming the first of what is now estimated to be the loss in excess of over 10,000 vessels on the Great Lakes. Compared to the obstacles met by the explorer LaSalle's *Griffin*, sailing the Great Lakes is now far less dangerous.

Modern materials, (fiberglass, dacron, nylon). electronic navigation, weather forecasts, accurate detailed charts, and the "iron kicker" (engine) all contribute to maximize a safe and successful journey on the still potentially dangerous Great Lakes. Compared to La Salle, the only thing I didn't have was time.

The Search for the Right Boat:

The search goes on constantly in that the boater is always reviewing new or used vessels in magazines, brochures, newspapers and boat yards.

I was fortunate in that I had a job that required extensive travel throughout the Great Lakes area. I was able to examine a number of used boats. Some of these experiences were frightening. There was the time a fellow wanted to show me a small 25-foot Coronado. We hopped into the cockpit and the owner immediately, much to my dismay, started the small inboard engine. "Don't you use a blower?" I asked* "Naw," came the response, "She doesn't have a blower. If you're careful, you don't need one." It was clear to me that I didn't want to acquire a boat from such a reckless individual.

Another boat examined was a 26-foot Columbia. I liked the boat and figured this could be my first deep water boat. It was a little smaller than I wanted, but would suffice as my first Lake Erie boat. I did not utilize a marine surveyor and was about to firm up a deal for purchase after one more inspection. While examining joints, sail lockers and every nook and cranny, I happen to discover that the wooden bulkhead had pulled away about one inch from the deck. This caused great concern and I elected not to proceed with the purchase.

One day I happened to pass a boat dealer located inland about twenty miles south of Lake Erie. This dealer primarily handled power-boats, but I think was attempting to get into sail boats. On display was a 28-foot sailboat manufactured by Tanzer, a Canadian company. I examined the boat carefully and determined this vessel would be safe and sea-worthy enough to manage the unexpected and potentially severe weather that occurs on the Great Lakes.

---

* Boats require a blower system to be turned on for several minutes before starting an engine. Fuel fumes are heavier than air and will settle to lower parts of the vessel. Running a blower system is a necessary safety precaution.

The following week I was on a business trip to Chicago and picked up a sailing magazine that listed and gave details of new sailboats for 1974. One of the boats listed was the Tanzer-28, the boat I had just examined. At this point I decided that this was the boat to be acquired.

When I returned to Cleveland I immediately went to the dealer and placed a $3000 deposit on the Tanzer. I agreed to pay the balance the following February. In the meantime the great fuel crunch of 1973-74 occurred and sailboat values jumped considerably. In February, I went to the dealer to pay the balance. The dealer took me aside and said, "I'll tell you what, I'll give you back your deposit of $3000 and a profit of $2000. Let me keep the boat."

When I rejected this offer the dealer said, "Where else can you make that kind of profit?" I told him, "Look, I've been looking for a boat for the last two years. I'm not interested in making a profit. I'm looking to take possession of the Tanzer." I christened the Tanzer, *Escape III.*

Escape III was a sturdy vessel. I was impressed with the fact that the fiberglass was thick and there was a heavy cast iron keel. Steering was controlled by the tiller, which attached directly to the rudder. Escape III came with a fore sail (jib) and a main sail. I shortly acquired a 170 % Genoa and a storm jib. The Genoa was 70% larger than the jib and hopefully would move the Escape III in relatively moderate wind. The storm jib is a fore sail considerably smaller than the jib. These three sails were attached to the forestay with hanks.

The size of the main sail was controlled by what is known as roller reefing, i.e. the boom holding the base or foot of the main sail is turned with a crank.

The area of the main sail area is reduced as it's lowered and twisted around the boom. The interior had standing room and was equipped with a porta-pottie, two- burner alcohol stove and a side opening ice box.*

The Tanzer was truly an international boat. The boat was manufactured in Canada, the sails (Ratsey & Lapthorn) were from England, the winches (Barlow) from Australia, and the two-cylinder gasoline 15 hp engine was from Sweden (Volvo-Penta).

In addition to getting the *Escape III* ready for launching I had to figure out where to keep her. Looking for a place to keep a boat involves numerous decisions. Initially, my major concerns were is the water deep enough; how far is the proposed location from the main body of water; are there local impediments to navigation; is the proposed location well protected from storm surges and flooding; how far is the proposed location from home? Coupled with these decisions were decisions such as selecting a marina or yacht club and associated costs. If a yacht club, what kind of club, party, social or working man (oops, I mean working person). Would I be paying for more than I required such as a swimming pool or tennis court?

Additional major concerns were to secure a safe place for the *Escape III,* comparatively near home. I finally settled on a well-protected yacht club fronting on Lake Erie

---

* A side opening ice-box is not as practical as a top loading ice-box. Every time the door is opened, cold air is lost.

adjacent to the mouth of the Chagrin River in Eastlake, Ohio, seventeen miles northeast of downtown Cleveland. *Escape III* was delivered to the Chagrin Lagoons Yacht Club in May of 1974.

Working on Escape III prior to launching.

As I was to find out, sailing out of Chagrin Lagoons, numerous individuals were to ask me the origin of the name "Chagrin". Having grown up on the east side of Cleveland and northeastern Ohio, chagrin seemed a common name such as the town of Chagrin Falls, a small town about twenty miles to the south of Lake Erie, or Chagrin Boulevard. As a youngster, I thought no more about the name chagrin than I did the names Painesville or Willoughby. Much to my chagrin, as I grew older, I eventually learned the definition of the word and had to come up with some reason why chagrin was so liberally applied to geographic names in the area, specifically the Chagrin River.

I have heard two explanations. One of these was when Moses Cleaveland, the founder of Cleveland, made his way along the south shore of Lake Erie looking for the river called Cuyahoga, meaning crooked in Indian lingo. He determined what is now the Chagrin River, much to his chagrin, was not the Cuyahoga. He thus named the river Chagrin. The other and most plausible explanation is, like the name Cuyahoga, an Indian word, which is the name of the river that slices through Cleveland, a corruption of an Indian word meaning "clear water". Who really knows the origin of the name, but these seemed to satisfy those inquirers.

I was now the proud owner of a displacement sailboat and a member of a yacht club. I found that I still had a number of things to learn about boaters.

Rag-baggers and Stink-potters:

Boating is comprised of a number of dichotomies. You either like boating or you don't. If you like boating, generally you prefer either a power boat (stink-potter) or a sail boat (rag-bagger). If you're a sailor, generally you prefer either cruising or racing. When I first joined a yacht club, most of the racing sailors insisted that I race. "Hell," I thought, "I'm in a race all week long. When I get aboard I want to relax and enjoy my vessel." Consequently, I became a cruising sailor.

This is not to say that the dichotomies exist apart from each other. Several years ago, my dock partner was the proud owner of an Owens 32 foot, twin-screw powerboat called *Pandora*. Elwood Sawitke, "Doc" (an optometrist), as he was affectionately referred to, was the Coast Guard Auxiliary, 9th District commander. Doc loved boating and, despite a significant difference in age, we became dear friends. Doc was of the "greatest generation" in that he was a Marine who served in the Pacific during World War II. Being a good-looking man with a chiseled face, he looked much like Admirable Bull Halsey. Instead of calling him Doc, I got into the habit of calling and referring to him as "Bull". The mutual advantage we had was that when we were at the club and the wind was blowing significantly, we'd go sailing. When there was little or no wind, we'd go out in *Pandora*. I remember one day when out on the *Pandora* Doc (Bull) said, "You know when I first started boating, I used to come out here (Lake Erie) and open her wide. Then I realized, why am I burning all that fuel when my objective is just to be out on the water?" No wonder he also liked to go sailing.

The enmity between rag-baggers and stink-potters is generally a good natured exchange such as "How can you stand traveling sixty miles in twelve hours when I can go the same distance in two and one-half hours?" My usual response was "If you're in a hurry, why not take an airplane?" There is the often given challenge by ragbaggers to stink-potters, "Wanna race?" Naturally the initial response is affirmative until the rag-bagger throws in the caveat, "Good, but let me determine the time and place." The rag-bagger will then offer an extended course where, if foul weather occurs, the stink-potter cannot run for shore and will be in a dangerous situation, while the rag-bagger will reduce sail and continue on his way. Another rag-bagger might suggest a course from Boston to Southampton, England.

This antagonism has existed since late in the nineteenth century when steam replaced sail. Very often some sailors not only appear, but actually are very hoity with regard to their boating brethren. "Anyone can hop into a power boat, turn on the engine and take off. To sail requires a special knowledge." Sometimes the power boater will come back with, "Sailors are just too cheap to buy fuel." In any event, to be a proficient and safe boater, both require an extensive knowledge of a multiple series of disciplines including navigation, weather, and rules of the road. While I have enjoyed this friendly exchange over the years, let me end this note by saying, some of my best friends are power-boaters.

The next challenge was to take the *Escape III* across Lake Erie. Bruce and I sailed across the lake to Rondeau Harbour, Ontario. We celebrated this accomplishment with a meal of canned beef stew and a bottle of wine. We spent the next six days sailing northeasterly into Canadian ports, back across the lake to Dunkirk, New York before returning to my new yacht club Chagrin Lagoons Y.C. (expounded herein "The First Navigation Challenge".)

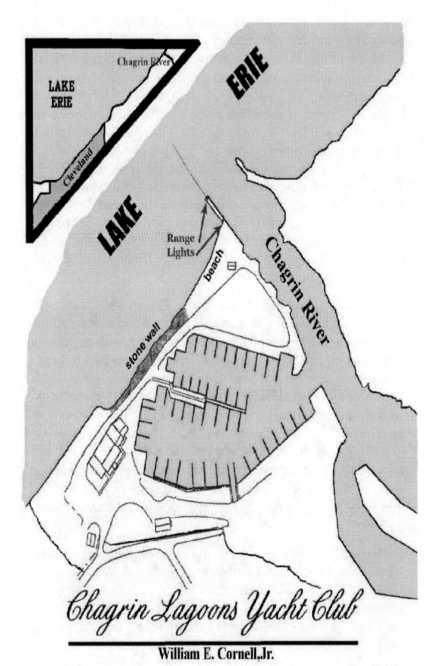

LAKE ERIE

Chagrin River

LAKE ERIE

Cleveland

ERIE

LAKE

Range Lights

beach

stone wall

Chagrin River

Chagrin Lagoons Yacht Club

William E. Cornell.,Jr.

The First Navigation Challenge

Every beginning yachtsman knows that someday he/she may be caught in a storm. For some, the fear of such a circumstance detracts from their continued boating pleasure and lurks over their shoulder as if a predator waiting to attack.

Still others seem oblivious to the possibility, taking unnecessary risks through a combination of ignorance and poorly found vessels. The fact is that storms do occur and any vessel venturing offshore is likely to be caught in a storm. The first storm could be a nightmare one may wish to not only survive, but also forget. Hopefully, it would be an experience on which to build.

My crewmember Bruce and I were well satisfied with our selves. After a year of planning and dreaming we had finally been able to concurrently take a weeks vacation and sail *Escape III* across Lake Erie. You would have thought we had conquered the Pacific Ocean such was our delight. Neither of us had ever cruised, with the exception of my completing the one-week bareboat charter in the British Virgin Island during the summer of 1972. More importantly, neither of us had ever been out of sight of land.

Bruce had crewed on my previous two boats. Slowly our knowledge and sailing skills had increased over the last two years through practice and study. Also, as mentioned previously, I had taken a correspondence navigation course in preparation for my bareboat charter in the Caribbean, and some Coast Guard and Power Squadron introductory courses.

Rondeau Harbour:

We departed Chagrin Lagoons at 0130 on Saturday, June 29, 1974. It was hazy and by 0500, the lights on the power company stacks located adjacent to the Chagrin Lagoons had disappeared. The haze continued as we slowly progressed northward under light air. During the earliest hours of the morning, I could barely make out the faint

An oreboat passes during the early hours of a misty morning.

outline of an ore boat gliding silently about three miles off our stern, evidence that we were crossing, or at least approaching, the mid-lake shipping lanes.

Our landfall was made early the next afternoon at Rondeau Harbour, Ontario, (Erieau, the adjacent town) a distance of approximately forty-six statute miles. The approach to the channel was greeted by the wailing sound of the diaphone at the harbor entrance. This was a welcome sound since the haze had continued to thicken. My thought, as we dropped sail and motored into the channel, was that of amazement at the accuracy of this first attempt at navigation without benefit of landmarks.

That evening, we enjoyed a sumptuous meal with a congratulatory bottle of wine and celebrated an accomplishment of paramount importance, if only to the two of us. We rested well, securely tied to one of the docks maintained by the Canadian government at the snug little harbor. Other than fishing boats, the only other boat at the government docks was an older thirty-five foot wooden powerboat from Lorain, Ohio.

The next day I introduced myself to the owner. Upon commenting on the fine condition of this older vessel, we were invited aboard and proudly given a tour. The vessel, which was built in 1927, was in mint condition below deck as well as above. With rattan chairs and couch the only indication that one had not stepped back in time was the radio equipment in the pilothouse.

I told the owner that we were going to leave shortly for Port Stanley located approximately fifty miles to the northeast along Lake Erie's northern shore. The owner responded that he was debating about returning to Lorain. He had three fishing companions who were supposed to return to work on Monday. It was beginning to blow and he was worried about some of his vessel's timbers now nearly a half-century old. He finally decided to remain at Rondeau Harbour until the weather improved.

Late in the morning, just before casting off, the owner of the aged vessel asked that we radio him to advise wind and wave conditions. We motored out the harbor channel into a southerly wind of about twenty knots and a four-foot swell directly into the channel. Once the channel was cleared, we took a forty-percent reef in the main and bent the storm jib.

It was beginning to rain and the waves were four to five feet. I radioed the owner of the aged vessel and briefly described the conditions. He thanked me for the information and announced that he was going to remain in Rondeau Harbour.

So far this was the most inclement weather that Bruce and I had experienced. We became quickly acclimated and began to thoroughly enjoy our condition as confidence in ourselves and *Escape III* continued to grow. Two hours under way the sound of the wind and waves was broken, at first intermittently, by a distant "rap, rap, rap". Our eyes scanned the horizon, but to no avail. Again, the sound was heard. Finally, we could see it. Just barely distinguishable in the distance a United States Coast Guard helicopter. The helicopter approached and circled. Bruce and I, in our foul-weather gear and safety harnesses, waved to indicate that we were well and in control. After circling and determining we were in no danger the helicopter was off in the direction from whence it came.

I have since learned that the helicopter was based in Mt Clemens, Michigan. I have often wondered what prompted the Coast Guard to check on us? Did they hear my call to the vessel at Rondeau Harbour and decide to check on us? Did they think finding us would be a good training exercise? It was comforting to know they were around. By evening the weather had moderated and we enjoyed a relaxing sail to Port Stanley, Ontario under full main and working jib.

Port Stanley:

Port Stanley is situated approximately fifty miles northeast of Rondeau Habour.

During darkness, lights can be somewhat confusing, especially to a comparatively novice sailor. During the darkness of the night we noticed a light glow on the horizon toward the Ontario shore. Could this be Port Stanley? The direction of the glow did not correspond with our original course. We initially headed for the light glow, but wisely, I decided to stay on our original course. We had commenced this twenty-three hour trip during stormy weather and concluded the voyage with a pleasant ten-knot wind under a clearing sky.

As we approached Port Stanley, again I was a little confused. The chart indicated large oil storage tanks. I assumed these would be white. As we got closer to the mouth of Kettle Creek and

Oil storage tanks off Port Stanley

Port Stanley, it turned out that the storage tanks were black making them difficult to see and recognize from the water.

Port Stanley was and still is accepting commercial bulk carriers. The entry to Kettle Creek was well marked with comparatively large buoys. As we made our way upstream it was apparent that Port Stanley was primarily a fishing village. Several blunt nosed fishing vessels were tied up in the outer harbor area. A bascule bridge blocked our way from going further upstream. The times of operation were posted on the bridge. We slowly circled the harbor and waited for the next scheduled opening of the bridge to proceed and make our way upstream.

The bridge finally opened. Just after passing the bridge someone yelled, "Hey, where you fellas going?" I yelled back, "Upstream looking for a dock." Why don't you dock here?" came the response. I circled the *Escape III* around and approached a pier jutting from the shore with about seven or eight docks for sailboats extending from each side of the pier. "You can tie off at the end of the pier." This was the Port Stanley Sailing Squadron. Since it was a weekday the area,

The bridge at Port Stanley as viewed from the Port Stanley Sailing Squadron

except for the guy who called to us, was deserted.

Having only six days vacation time remaining, we had a tentative schedule that required our departure early the next day. The weather forecast called for the possibility of rain with locally heavy winds within storms. We timed our departure in the morning with the opening of the bridge and proceeded down Kettle Creek under conditions far more favorable than our departure from Rondeau Harbour. The sky was overcast and the wind was from the south at ten to fifteen knots. I planned to get about five miles off shore and sail for Long Point Light at the eastern end of Long Point about sixty miles east of Port Stanley, then north-north-west across Long Point Bay to Port Dover.

Two hours out, the wind began to pick up. We had sailed southeast since I wanted to get some sea room if any of the storms caught us. The waves began to pick up from the south at about four to five feet. Sporadically it would rain, which had a brief calming effect on the surface.

Bringing the *Escape III* into the wind, Bruce and I climbed forward to lower the working jib, reef the main and again bend the storm jib. Several weeks prior, while on a shake down cruise and exposed to some heavy wind, I bent the storm jib without reefing the main. This imbalanced the *Escape III* and gave her a strong weather helm. I struggled against this condition and finally realized the necessity of reefing the main when using the storm jib to achieve balance.

At this time Bruce had experimented with wrapping his safety line around the mast while standing in front of the mast with his back to the bow. This gave him a degree of stability on a pitching deck and freed his hands for roller reefing the mainsail. Bruce was using this method as I bent the storm jib to the forestay.

Increasingly the wind blew as we made our way back to the cockpit. By this time the rain began to have a stinging sensation. The rain then stopped and yet the intensity of the wind continued to increase, as the waves grew larger. Seven-feet, eight-feet, nine-feet. The tops of the waves were being ripped from the surface and spindrift spread unevenly into the troughs and wave crests. One of the caps on a shroud turnbuckle cover came loose and was blown more than half way up the shroud, yet another indicator of the strength and velocity of wind.

We struggled with the tiller in an attempt to keep twenty degrees off the wind, despite the pressure of nine-foot waves. I wanted to continue our southward progress away from shore now about seven miles off our port quarter. This also prevented hitting the waves head on and made *Escape III* ride more easily. Occasionally, however, in the confused turbulence of the water, *Escape III* would hit bow on and fall into a trough with a shudder or be slammed abeam. This disruption of the wave pattern was evidence of another possible distant storm or the imperfect wave development due to Lake Erie's relative shallowness.

Still the intensity of the wind continued to grow. The air was alive with a roaring sound. Aside from wind and wave, the only other sound was the occasional slamming of the hull into a trough. With the exception of a semi-rhythmic wave pattern from the south, southwest, the surface of the lake was boiling wildly as Bruce and I took short turns at the tiller. Neither of us made comment about what was happening. Somehow verbal communication, while nearly impossible, seemed out of place. Neither of us wanted to break the hypnotic effect of oneness the storm had achieved by blending wind, wave, vessel, crew, sky and water.

The trance was broken when the hull again slammed into a trough. I was suddenly jolted into consciousness and found the storm invigorating as well as frightening. Would the storm continue to build? How could it? Would the rigging continue to hold? As each wave approached the bow was buried after which it lifted only to drop again and again.

My confidence in *Escape III* and our ability to maintain control under such adverse conditions was steadily growing. I kept cautioning myself not to become over confident. After all, we were only in a holding action against the elements.

Imperceptibly the wind began to subside. For a while the water's surface continued in a tumultuous state before it too began to subside. We were finally able to get back on course still carrying the reefed main and storm jib. By late afternoon we spotted the north shore. It was still overcast and the moderated wind continued out of the south. By early evening we were able to un-reef the main and raise the working jib. Soon we would be making our way along Long Point peninsula.

At 2400 the new day arrived accompanied by the sound of the foghorn at Long Point. This solitary sound and light warns shipping to stay to the south and avoid the Long Point peninsula and the confine of Long Point Bay. Long Point peninsula protrudes about fifteen miles east, south-east from the Canadian shore. A danger to vessels is evidenced by the multitude of shipwrecks that have occurred along Long Point peninsula. Across our starboard beam the shipping lane was void of any major activity except a tug-boat. The tug flashed a spotlight on us as if to say, "What in hell are you doing out here at this time?"

Port Dover:

We rounded the point and set course for Port Dover across Long Point Bay. The bay was comparatively rough and we were now in a following sea with *Escape III* yawing back and forth as we made our way north, northwest. At 0200 we spotted the mid-channel flashing "A" buoy. We continued on course straining to see lighted buoys and the range lights that would indicate a safe passage into Port Dover. Seeing theses lights was difficult due to backscatter of other lights. This was to be my first night time landfall and I wanted it to be uneventful.

As we entered the channel, Port Dover was deserted except for a few persons fishing off the government wharf. Our passage up the Lynn River was blocked by a bridge, which was not operating at this time of the morning. I decided to tie off a fishery wharf along the east bank. With our lines secured, Bruce and I collapsed into our bunks, the silence broken only by gusts of wind whistling through nearby trees. This had been my first night landing and series of storms. I knew they would not be the last.

The Lynn River at Port Dover.

After a few hours sleep we were awakened by carts being pushed along the wharf. Commercial fishing boats were unloading. While we were in the way, no one complained, yelled or chased us off. Perhaps they realized we had arrived exhausted from the recent weather conditions and were tied up in the dark at the first available wharf. Not wishing to interfere with men working for a living, we cast off and made our way up the Lynn River to the Port Dover Yacht Club. We then spent the remainder of the day wandering in the very pleasant downtown area of Port Dover.

The following day we departed for Dunkirk, New York at 0800. Dunkirk was selected as an objective since Bruce's mother lived there. This was a pleasant forty-three mile sail with a fifteen-knot wind out of the southwest, perfect for our southeast course. We arrived at Dunkirk after a twelve-hour sail. Bruce immediately called his mother. Shortly thereafter, we enjoyed an excellent home cooked meal.

Becalmed:

The following day we departed at 0700 as Mrs. Washington waved goodbye to us. Initially, we tacked since the wind was still at fifteen knots, but now out of the west, southwest. By the time we were off Presque Isle, Erie, Pennsylvania, the wind had died and we were becalmed. At this time I was not only a sailor, but a die-hard sailor. Sailboats were meant to be sailed. Auxiliary engines were meant to be used for getting into and out of port. We sat in the dark for six hours without a breath of wind. "Think I'll catch a few zzzzs," Bruce said as he went below.

There I sat alone in the dark when I began to notice a strange phenomenon. The sky to the north began to look like it was on fire. Not a burning fire, but rather waves of light blue, green, and gray. Was the earth coming to the end? "Hey Bruce, better get up here and take a look at this." Bruce came up through the companionway, looked up toward the north and exclaimed, "Wow! The northern lights. I haven't seen those for years." Whew! This made sense and it was comforting to know that the world wasn't coming to an end.

We sat several hours longer until the northern lights dissipated. Finally, I had to give up being a stubborn, die-hard sailor. Thank God for the little two-cylinder Volvo-Penta engine. We spent the next eleven hours motoring along Lake Erie's southeast shore and returned to Chagrin Lagoons.

During this initial cruise, I learned that I was capable of navigating on the waters of Lake Erie, the *Escape III* was a sound vessel, and Lake Erie is an extremely fickle and often unpredictable body of water with rapidly changing weather ranging from severe storms to long periods of windless calms. Little did I know that Port Stanley and its people would become my favorite port on the Great Lakes.

Now that I was familiar with Lake Erie the next challenge would be to take on the Welland Canal that bypasses the Niagara River and Niagara Falls and permits transit into Lake Ontario. Bruce and I accomplished this in 1976. (expounded in "Seaway Welland-This is *Escape III*")

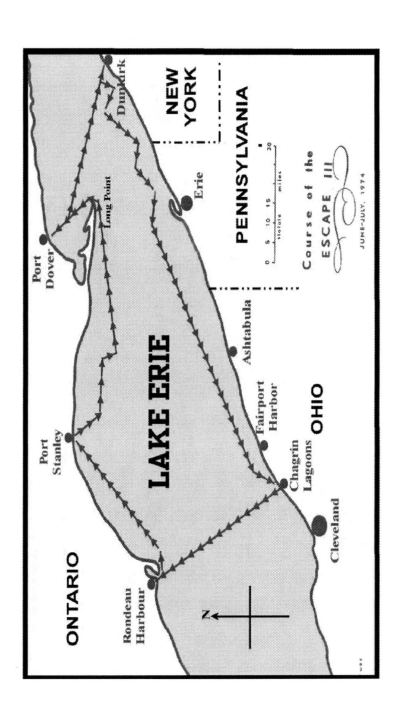

ONTARIO

Port
Dover

Long Point

Port
Stanley

Rondeau
Harbour

LAKE ERIE

Dunkirk

NEW
YORK

Erie

PENNSYLVANIA

Ashtabula

Fairport
Harbor

Chagrin
Lagoons

OHIO

Cleveland

N

Course of the
ESCAPE III
JUNE-JULY, 1974

0   5   10   15   30
        statute   miles

"Seaway Welland, This is *Escape III*"

For two summers I had sailed Lake Erie. Rondeau Harbour, Port Stanley, Port Dover, Dunkirk, Conneaut, and Fairport Harbor: all knew the *Escape III*, which, had proven her mettle in the short chop brought forth by Lake Erie's shallowness. Once again I was transiting Lake Erie only this time my objective was beyond Lake Erie's shores. Toronto, Canada was calling. I had been to Toronto several times. My wife's maternal Grandparents, uncle and cousins lived there. This necessitated numerous visits over the years and I was anxious to see the city from the water.

Bruce, my sailing companion, and I were now determined to sail beyond Lake Erie to Toronto on Lake Ontario. Such a trip would require transit through the Welland Canal.

The Welland Canal is a man made waterway that bypasses the Niagara River and Niagara Falls and permits shipping to pass from Lake Erie with an elevation of 570 feet to Lake Ontario with an elevation of 245 feet. The first canal was constructed in the 1820s and completed with forty locks in 1829. As Great Lakes vessels increased in size a second canal with 27 locks was opened in 1840 followed by a third canal with 26 locks opening in 1887. The fourth canal with 8 locks was opened in 1932 and remains in use today.

Downbound:

We departed from the Chagrin River at 0100 on a Saturday, July 10, 1974 on a northeast course. The sky was overcast and a light wind was out of the south. At 0530 a light rain accompanied by lightening and a freshening wind dictated a sail change. I climbed onto the foredeck, dropped the Genoa and bent the storm jib. By 0900 the wind continued to increase to 30+ knots with a heavy downpour. Bruce climbed onto the foredeck to reef the mainsail as we continued our northeast course toward the eastern extension of Long Point peninsula. At 1200 the waves had grown to ten feet as the wind began to slacken and the sky began to clear.

We finally spotted the Canadian shore at 1430 and Long Point light at 1615. I was exceptionally pleased at seeing the Long Point light directly on the bow after a 90 mile sail. At this time this was my longest sail by purely dead reckoning.*

After passing Long Point light, we continued our northeast course toward Port Colborne located about 45 miles distant at the south end of the Welland Canal. At 0800 again it was clouding over and the wind was exceptionally light. We ran the engine for about one hour to charge the battery. Gradually, the wind picked up to 5 knots from the southwest. Bruce decided to go below for a snooze as occasional small storms moved westward.

While Bruce was below I had a very unusual experience. Prior to leaving on this voyage I had been on a business trip to Minneapolis. The Friday I returned to Cleveland I had started the day at 6:00 a.m. By this time I had been awake for about 40 hours. As I sat at the helm I began to doze off, jerk into consciousness as my chin fell to my chest, doze off, jerk into consciousness, doze off trying desperately to keep a compass heading. All of a sudden, I was hallucinating and saw a steel girder in front of *Escape III* in the middle of Lake Erie. I knew I couldn't continue and called Bruce up from below. Strangely, when Bruce and I changed places, I could rest, but not sleep. I can only

---

* Dead reckoning is determining a position based on time, speed, distance and direction from a known or estimated location.

attribute this to adrenalin and the anticipation of the prospect of going into the Welland Canal.

It was 0300 when we followed a "salty"[*] into the mouth of the Port Colborne harbor. The "salty" tied up at one of the entrance wharfs as we motored past anxious to make contact with "Seaway Welland" and commence our down bound transit. About 200 yards before the canal entrance a sign directed us further into the canal and to a public docking area. It was here that pleasure vessels were to contact "Seaway Welland" by radio or a telephone located at the edge of the dock.

When several boating friends heard that I was going to go to Toronto via the Welland Canal the advice mounted rapidly. "You have to have several fifty-foot lines." "They require you to have burlap bags full of straw for protection against the sides of the locks." "They make you wait until they can pack 30 boats together." "The transit through the canal will take twenty-four hours."

Now, I would know first hand the horrors of entering the canal. With great trepidation I tuned my radio to channel 14, grabbed the microphone and in my best seamanlike voice said, "Seaway Welland, this is the pleasure craft *Escape III* requesting instructions for down bound transit, over." The response was immediate. "*Escape III* this is Seaway Welland. What is your length, draft, tonnage and how many persons are onboard?"

After responding with the proper information, Seaway Welland came back and instructed me to keep the radio on and await further instructions. Within a few minutes Seaway Welland announced that they had an up bound freighter and would enter Lock #8 shortly. Were we ready to cast of? My God, we just got here. I needed time to collect my thoughts. "Yes, we'll be ready to cast off in ten

---

[*]"Salty" Descriptive word used to distinguish ocean vessels from Great Lakes freighters.

minutes." Seaway Welland responded "O.K." and warned that if we didn't make this lock, we probably would have to wait several hours. The message was clear. "Hey Bruce we have to cast off in ten minutes or we'll have to wait several hours. Let's get ready." Get ready how? No sooner had I said it than I realized we were ready.

Within a few minutes Seaway Welland called and asked us to move to a wall along our starboard side just outside Lock #8. We moved into position accordingly and waited for the lock gates to open and issue the up bound freighter. Seaway Welland then contacted the freighter and announced, "When exiting there will be a pleasure craft to your port, but he knows what he's doing." It seemed my best seamanlike voice had been acceptable.

Lock #8 was the first lock to be entered for down bound traffic. The lock does not have a significant drop in that its purpose is to regulate and provide a level based on Lake Erie's variable level. Lock #8 was the first lock to be entered for down bound traffic. At the direction of Seaway Welland we entered the lock and floated freely without lines as the lock gate behind us closed and we were lowered two or three feet. At 0430 the opposite gate opened and we proceeded to Lock #7 approximately 17 miles to the north.

As we motored along the canal daylight approached and began to burn off a light fog. We found our selves in a rural setting accompanied by an occasional red-wing-black bird in the

An up bound lake freighter passes during a misty morning.

adjacent fields. No pleasure craft were noted. However, we did come across lake freighters as they made their way up bound to Lake Erie. At midmorning we came to Lock #7.

Bruce climbed ashore and tied off while waiting for the gate to open and instruction to enter. This lock had a significant drop as it was positioned at the Niagara escarpment as were Locks #6. #5. and #4 found a little

A quick snooze before entering a lock.

further down. As we entered the lock, lock workers passed lines to us as the gate to the rear closed. *Escape III* settled to the lower level, the gate opened and we were off at the lower level to Lock #6.

Lock #6 was a short distance and abuts Locks #5 and #4. In other words after the drop in Lock #6, exit is made directly into Lock #5, after which the drop in Lock #5, exit is made directly into Lock #4. Again lock workers passed lines to us in each successive lock. It is at these three locks payment is made to one of the lock masters. The cost was $3.00 per lock or $24.00 for passage through the Welland Canal. Locks #3, #2 and #1 were spaced one to two miles from each other beyond lock #4.

We exited the canal at about 1300 having made the twenty-six mile trip in 8 ½ hours. Transit through the canal, contrary to all the advice and warnings given by

Downbound out of a lock

fellow boaters, did not require anything other than patience, following instructions, fenders and utilizing lines provided by the Seaway Welland Authority.

While motoring the last portion of the canal we stopped to off load the dinghy. Once in the water I put the *Escape III* into gear and proceeded to get the dinghy painter (line) wrapped around the propeller and shaft. As a consequence, the engine came to an abrupt halt. What a place for this to happen, a main entry channel into the Welland Canal? Something had to be done and fast. I grabbed a knife and slid into the water and proceeded to cut the line away from the propeller and shaft. Fortunately, I was able to complete this task before we became an obstacle to navigation or were run down by a freighter.

It was another 30 plus miles across Lake Ontario to Toronto. By 1500 heavy rain fell for about ½ hour as we made our way north, northwest finally spotting the CN Tower. The wind was beginning to shift to the northwest. We now had to tack in order to make headway to our objective.

Slowly the magnificent Toronto skyline came into view with the dominating CN Tower. This 1815 foot tall edifice was just completed in 1976. At the time, it was the tallest structure in the world, a record it held for over thirty years. The Tower is visible for several miles and makes for easy navigation at this western end of Lake Ontario.

As we approached Toronto we decided to find dockage at Ontario Place. Now under power, we rounded Gibraltar Point located at the southeastern tip of the island complex found adjacent to Toronto's waterfront and headed for Ontario Place. Ontario Place consists of three man made islands devoted to an amusement park and a public marina. We pulled up to the marina entrance at 1930 and were informed that dockage was unavailable. "What'll we do now?" questioned Bruce. By this time we were quickly running out of daylight and energy. We had been traveling about forty-two hours. I went below to check the chart for potential docking possibilities. I came up and told Bruce, "There's a National Yacht Club about ¾ mile to the northeast. Let's go over there and see if we can dock."

We turned to the northeast entered a through a narrow break-wall opening into a mooring basin and crossed to the National Yacht Club. At 2030 we tied off in front of the clubhouse. Being Sunday evening the area was deserted.

"You want a scotch?" I asked Bruce. "Of course," came the response. After pouring a couple of stiff drinks we climbed a stairway at the side of the clubhouse. We sat down on a patio overlooking the mooring basin and *Escape III.* We were relieved to be safely tied up. Exhaustion soon after dictated the requirement for sleep. We had traveled over 200 miles in just over forty-three hours.

The next morning we were in for a surprise. We had tied up with the starboard side toward the clubhouse landing. At the stern a portion of the landing ended and commenced about ten feet toward the club house. During the night the starboard bow-line  had come loose and Escape III made a 180 degree swing so that the port side was now along the landing. "Hey Bruce, I could have sworn we tied up with the starboard side toward the landing." Bruce said, "We did. The starboard bow line must have come loose and we swung around 180 degrees."

We had made arrangement to meet our wives Carol and Debbie in Toronto after they had driven from Ohio. As mentioned previously, my wife had family in Toronto and we soon called them at her uncle's home. Shortly thereafter, Carol and Debbie came to meet us at the National Yacht Club.

Toronto:

It was fortuitous that we were unable to find dockage at Ontario Place. A short walk from the National Yacht Club was the Molson brewery, which we toured, and public transportation. Some members of the club recommended several nightspots and restaurants. We spent a week exploring tourist attractions such as Casa Loma a castle like mansion built by a Canadian industrialist in the early 1900s; enjoying the friendliness of the National Yacht Club; and experiencing the international flavor of the metropolitan area. Three specific events stand out in my memory.

One day were taking it easy at the club. The weather was overcast and rainy. Some club members came in extremely upset. The club commodore had just been motoring his boat down a nearby channel to a place to step his mast. He was struck by lightening and instantly killed. That his mast was not up he did not have what is known as a cone of protection.

One late afternoon we entered a Chinese restaurant. Much to our surprise we were the only occidentals in the restaurant. Shortly, a woman came over and handed us menus listing 30 or 40 dishes, written in Chinese. When our server came over to take our order, we looked at her with apparent confusion. She smiled and said in a very oriental accent, "You not been to -------Gardens?" One or all of us responded negatively. She smiled again and said, "I order for you," to which we agreed. She returned shortly with six bowls of dishes served family style. When finished, she presented us with a check written in Chinese. I thought that probably we were being taken to the Chinese cleaners. We were not.

The third memorable incident occurred when one evening we went to a recommended nightspot, which sported a jazz band. Upon leaving the nightspot an exceptionally inebriated couple walked out with us. As we were waiting for a streetcar to pass, the young lady stepped into the path of the on coming streetcar. I grabbed her to pull her back at which time her companion ready to fight yelled, "Hey, mother (expletive), that's my wife." He calmed down when I turned and said, "Good, and that's my wife." We continued on without incident.

Back to Sailing:

After a week of such excitement, were ready to return to the comparative calm of the Great Lakes. Now at least we had some idea of the Welland Canal. We said goodbye to the wives and departed the National Yacht Club at 1730. It was partly cloudy with the wind out of the west at fifteen to twenty knots. We raised the main and working jib and spotted the Lake Ontario south shore at 1900.

We entered Port Weller at the north end of the canal and contacted Seaway Welland. At 0115 we entered Lock #1 and were instructed to pull all the way forward into the lock. This time we were not going to lock through by ourselves. Instead, a Russian freighter pulled in behind us. It was frightening and intimidating to see the freighter bow move up on us.

Going up bound in the locks is a little more difficult than going down bound. As water is permitted to flow into the lock, a swirling current must be dealt with and *Escape III* kept from banging against the concrete wall. We locked with the Russian freighter all the way through Lock #7 at which time the freighter docked at St. Catherines.

We now continued alone through the remaining seventeen miles to Lock #8 during the early hours of the morning. As mentioned previously, this lock does not have a significant change in level since its purpose is to regulate a level based on Lake Erie's variable level. After exiting the lock at 1015 and Seaway Welland Control we tied up at the Port Colborne wharf behind a pilot boat.

This time we were able to transit the canal in nine hours. We were now ready for a short three-hour nap. In the afternoon we were invited aboard the pilot boat by the captain. He told us that the freighters, ore boats and saltys were all required to have a pilot aboard when transiting the canal. He further explained that piloting was an exceptionally coveted job since the pilots were well paid and had the advantage of being able to sleep in their own beds. He also explained that pilots had very stringent requirements such as having at least ten years experience as a sea captain.

The pilot boat at Port Colborne

We spent the remainder of the day conversing with the pilot boat captain interrupted by his occasional trips out to off shore vessels to drop off or pick up pilots. That evening, exhaustion again overtook us and we slept thirteen hours.

After a breakfast, we departed Port Colborne at 0900 under an overcast sky. The wind was above thirty knots. We reefed the main and used the storm jib as we attempted to make our way southwest again toward Long Point light.

Eight-foot waves and a southwest wind prevented a direct course and we were forced to tack for several hours. Finally, at 1900 the wind slackened to fifteen knots and we were able to un-reef the main and bend the working jib, still tacking into a southwest wind.

At 2230 Long Point light was spotted. Shortly thereafter, a blinding and prolonged rain began to fall. I was fearful of heading toward Long Point, which now could not be seen and also fearful of heading too far south into the shipping lanes with greatly reduced visibility. The water flattened from the pounding rain and the wind was barely perceptible. We drifted somewhere northeast of the end of Long Point taking turns in the cockpit watching the dimmed bulkhead mounted compass as a heavy rain continued during the dark hours.

Just before 0600 the rain subsided and I was able to pick up the radio direction finder signal of Long Point. We slowly powered toward Long Point light and finally at 0730 spotted the light tower barely visible in a light misty fog. The wind had shifted to the east and we again went under sail with less than one hundred miles to go.

For the remainder of the day, evening and well into the next morning we continued under sail with a clear sky, a moderate wind of ten to fifteen knots now out of the northeast. We tied up at Chagrin Lagoons Yacht Club at 0615. Since leaving Port Colborne we had traveled approximately 165 miles in a little over forty-five hours.

Most importantly, we had entered another great lake, conquered the, heretofore unknown, Welland Canal and learned not to listen to the hearsay stories of other boaters.

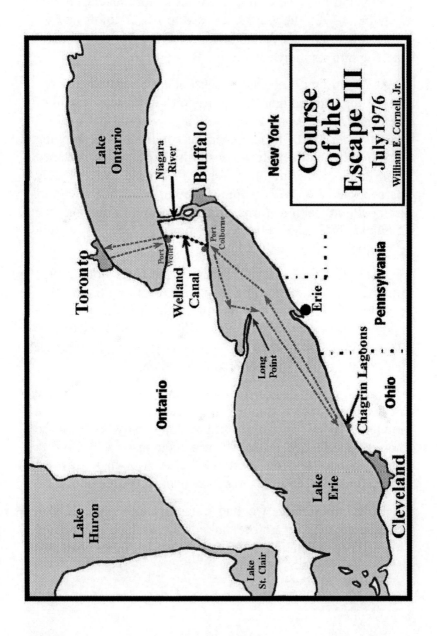

Course of the
Escape III
July 1976
William E. Cornell, Jr.

New York

Pennsylvania

Ohio

Ontario

Lake Ontario

Lake Huron

Lake St. Clair

Lake Erie

Toronto

Buffalo

Niagara River

Welland Canal

Port Weller

Port Colborne

Erie

Long Point

Chagrin Lagoons

Cleveland

The *Mistress:*

A Good Excuse

I began to consider a new boat partially because of an incident that occurred on my Tanzer. I really loved the Tanzer that for four years carried me all over Lake Erie, thru the Welland Canal and across Lake Ontario to Toronto. One day at the gas dock of my yacht club I was preparing to fuel up when I told Bruce, "Put the boards in the companion way." He looked at me like I was crazy and said. "What for?" I explained to him that gas fumes are heavy and if the boat was not closed up, the heavier fumes could make their way into the lower section of the hull and explained further that a quarter cup of vaporized gasoline had the explosive power of four sticks of dynamite. Bruce was not quite convinced, but followed instructions.

Once the boards were in I began taking on fuel. When finished, I told Bruce to remove the companionway boards and check below while I paid for the gas. He came back up through the companionway with a very disturbed look and said, "You better take a look. I smell gasoline." I jumped below and removed a bilge board only to find about a quarter inch of gasoline floating in the bilge. I had to find out immediately where the gasoline was leaking into the bilge. I gave a bucket and sponge to Bruce to get rid of the bilge fuel while I removed the engine (the 2 cylinder Volvo-Penta) cover to determine the source of the fuel leak. Looking over the engine carefully, I noticed that a clamp on the fuel vent line mounted on the inside of the transom at the rear of the engine compartment had come loose and allowed fuel to leak into the bilge.

Realizing that I had to fix this problem immediately. I got a new clamp and crawled back into the narrow area between the engine and hull. I reached up, placed the clamp to the reattached vent line and was to about tighten the clamp with a screwdriver. I stopped. What if there was a static spark? The whole thing would blow up and I would die. If, by chance, I didn't die immediately, I would be trapped in that narrow engine compartment. Stop and think, I thought to myself. You have on a pair of cotton jeans and a cotton T-shirt. Shouldn't be a static spark. Well, no static spark. After crawling out of the engine compartment and gaining my composure I said, "I'm going to get another boat and this time with a diesel engine."

Boat owners usually dream of a bigger boat and the fuel incident was just enough of an excuse to start thinking of and searching for a replacement of the Tanzer. Again, the search for a new boat ritual began. The intensity increased with perusal of a multiple number of yachting magazines, sending away for brochures, attending boat shows, and examining and inspecting as many boats as possible.

A friend at the yacht club had acquired a Tartan 37, which he named *Taboo*. "Hey Helmut, how do you like your new Tartan?" As is generally the case with boaters, Helmut was anxious to proudly show me his new possession and invited me below. I must say I was quite impressed. "How does she sail?" I asked. In a thick German accent Helmut said, "She sails beautifully. We (his wife Ilssa and daughter Connie) are planning a trip to the islands* next weekend. Would you and your family like to go along and you can see for yourself?" This was an invitation I could not turn down. We took the trip the following weekend.

---

* The Islands refer to a cluster of islands located in the southwest portion of Lake Erie among them South Bass, Middle Bass, Kellys and Pelee Island.

While I had been following the ritual described above (intensively reading about and examining bigger boats), I knew, after this trip, the Tartan 37 was exactly what I had been looking for. The size and layout were sufficient for my needs. The Tartan manufacturing plant was only ten miles northeast along the lake at a community called Grand River. I reasoned that if I had any problems with a new boat, it would be advantageous to have the manufacturer nearby.

That fall I purchased a Tartan 37 that I promptly named *Mistress*. My wife's only comment with regard to the name was, "With what you paid for that boat, you couldn't afford another mistress."

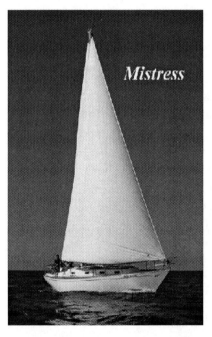

The *Mistress* came equipped with standard interior lighting, navigation lights, sails (a main sail and a 150% Genoa jib sail), a 40 horsepower Westerbeke diesel engine, a Ritchie compass mounted in the binnacle, winches and standard hardware and rigging required for this sail boat. In addition, the rigging included roller furling that permitted the Genoa to furl around the head stay like a window blind. The interior had a head, two cabins (convertible to 7 bunks) and, most important to me, a navigator's station.

Conveniences included a three-burner alcohol (non-explosive) stove, a top loading icebox with no refrigeration, and a two-bowl sink. The only luxury was a pressurized hot/cold water system.

Instruments:

I equipped the Mistress with the following basic instruments; a depth sounder, a combined wind speed indicator (anemometer) and wind direction indicator[*], distance log and speed indicator. The distance log[**] is a small paddle wheel positioned through the hull and spins as the vessel moves through the water and electronically transfers the speed to a gauge.

These along with the compass would hopefully permit me to navigate safely anywhere on the Great Lakes or the world, for that matter.

The combined anemometer and wind direction sensors and the radio antenna were mounted on the masthead with wiring running down through the mast.

Where the wiring exited the mast there is a connecter panel on the main cabin bulkhead to connect the mast wires with the instruments. A boat yard employee instead ran the wires to a small connecter panel he mounted on a stringer in the bilge. "Why didn't you put the connections in the bulkhead connecter box where they should have been?" The employee was caught and said, "It's too late now. I already cut the wires." This taught me a lesson. Don't let someone work on your boat if you can do it yourself and if you can't do it yourself, make sure you closely supervise the work. In

---

[*]Wind speed is measured using spinning cups and wind direction vane both usually mounted at the top of the mast. Unless at a dock or at anchor, the registered speed and direction are slightly enhanced by the forward motion of the vessel resulting in what is referred to as apparent wind.

[**] Techniques and instruments for measuring distance have been around for years. Originally in determining speed, sailing ships would use a line knotted at intervals connected to a resistance float. When trailed in the water from the stern, the knotted line would be paid out so that the speed could be determined. Thus, the origin of the term knots when referring to speed. Later, a more sophisticated instrument with a small propeller was towed that turned the line attached to a numerical counter.

later years, I was able to install additional items such as a self-steering device, refrigeration, and navigation devices. Apologies to the reputable, conscientious boat yards and boat yard employees.

I also equipped the *Mistress* with certain tools and electronic items such as the radio and radio direction finder previously utilized on the *Escape III.*

Mistress was now ready to be delivered to Chagrin Lagoons where she would dock next to Helmut's sister vessel the *Taboo.* At the time, little did I realize that the *Mistress* and I would spend the next thirty years together. Extensive cruises to Lake Huron, Georgian Bay, Lake Superior and Lake Ontario were added to the log of the *Mistress* beginning with the voyage I refer to herein as *Seven Days to Nowhere.*

Mistress's First Crossing to Port Stanley:

Mistress settled into the yacht club in June of 1978 and I was anxious to cross Lake Erie to Port Stanley. My former dock partner (because of increased length I had to secure a longer dock) Doc (Bull) Sawitke agreed to accompany me on this maiden voyage. The crossing went well. After spending the night at Port Stanley, having breakfast at the "Lake View" restaurant, and listening to a weather report we departed early in the morning back across the lake to Chagrin Lagoons.

While what seemed to be a perfect sail, all of a sudden, the large Genoa came loose from the masthead and fell to the deck and partially into the water. Doc and I rushed forward. The Genoa is large and we struggled to pull it aboard and stuff it into the forward hatch. I later determined that the head of the sail was attached with a screw shackle, which came unscrewed. This was to later be replaced with a more secure snap shackle.

We made our way back to the cockpit and continued to sail under main sail alone. The sky was overcast but did not appear threatening. Suddenly, the wind dramatically increased. Doc and I sat in the cockpit until I told him to go below. As he did so I noticed on the anemometer that the wind was now blowing at forty knots. I yelled above the screaming wind, "Put the companionway boards in." Doc yelled back, "Are you sure? If this thing goes over, I'll be trapped inside." "Doc, she's not going to go over, and if she did keeping boards in will keep her from sinking."

Still, the wind continued to blow, with the anemometer pointer often being pegged at sixty knots. By now I was struggling with a full main and trying to dump air to stay reasonably upright. The cockpit was full of water with the engine instruments completely submerged.

Doc slid the companionway hatch partially open and popped his head out. "Do you think we ought to listen to a weather forecast?" I yelled back to overcome the noise of the wind, "Who cares what the weather forecast says? We're in it now." With that, Doc closed the hatch as I continued to battle the storm.

Over a period of four hours, from about 0800 to 1200, the wind never went below forty knots and bounced often to sixty plus knots. Finally, the wind began to ameliorate and by 12:30 it was over. Doc now had a chance to listen to the weather radio. "Occasional scattered periods of rain with accompanying gusting winds."

Fortunately, there was no significant damage except for a twisted goose-neck fitting. The following week I took the fitting to Tartan. The fellow I showed the fitting to said, "Better to bend rather than break." About two weeks later, Tartan sent me a redesigned beefed up goose-neck* fitting, which never failed me over the next thirty years.

---

* A goose-neck fitting is a piece of hardware, which connects the boom to the mast.

Relevant Digressions

Before I begin relaying some additional circumstances of the voyages of the *Mistress*, clarifying groundwork should be outlined to fully comprehend further presentations. They are: Mr. Singer; a first mate for nearly thirty years; the observations of freighters; and Port Stanley, my favorite port.

Mr. Singer:

Shortly after I had acquired the *Mistress* I met Mr. William Earnest Singer. The previous year Mr. Singer had jumped ship from another vessel (the *Taboo*, sister yacht to my own Tartan 37). I've never been sure why he made the switch, but I've never been sorry or disappointed. At the time Mr. Singer was a welder with an unbelievably broad education resulting from a high school education at a local

private boys school. Mr. Singer had been sailing around Lake Erie on several other, mostly racing, boats. Thus, he understood and reveled in the concept of making a vessel move from place to place using wind power.

Having a wiry physic, Mr. Singer enjoyed prancing around the deck, raising sail, coiling lines, and all those miscellaneous chores required on a sailing vessel. In addition, Mr. Singer was an excellent natural mechanic who was able to advise and assist in any necessary repairs and the installation of equipment. Mr. Singer was always there whether it be to work on getting the boat into the water or sailing off, day or night.

One of Mr. Singer's major characteristics was that he was not a conversationalist of brevity. When discussing any subject, Mr. Singer could go on and on and into detail beyond the requirement of the subject being discussed, particularly when how to perform a mechanical repair, or a welding project. Interestingly, Mr. Singer's description of a project would increase proportionately with the amount of beer consumed. For me, this was a perfect attribute of a shipmate since my interest in any subject discussed, increased proportionately with the amount of beer I consumed.

There was one area where Mr. Singer's tendency to elaborate did not function. This was when he referred to me. During all coming the years in which we sailed together, I can never remember Mr. Singer calling me anything except "Corn" while I got into the habit of calling William Earnest Singer, "Mr. Singer." It should be noted that these names were utilized regardless of the amount of beer consumed.

It appeared that we would be compatible shipmates. Little did I realize that Mr. Singer would be my first-mate during the next thirty-years.

Great Lakes Freighters:

Two kinds of freighters are found in the Great Lakes. Lakers, sometimes called ore boats, are bulk carriers that primarily carry iron ore from the Mesabi iron ore range in Minnesota to steel making industrial centers such as Gary, Indiana; the River Rouge area near Detroit, Michigan; Cleveland, Ohio; Buffalo, New York and Hamilton,

Ontario. Even though they also carried coal, limestone, salt, gypsum, cement and some agricultural (primarily grain) products, they are often generally referred to as ore boats.

"Salties" are ocean-going freighters that come into the Great Lakes from the Atlantic Ocean via the St. Lawrence Seaway. The earlier (1862) canal on the St. Lawrence River permitted transit of vessels less than 200 feet to Lake Ontario. At the same time the Welland Canal was limited to vessels of less than 150 feet and permitted transit of vessels into the upper lakes.

A salty enters a Seaway lock.

In 1959, the presently existing St. Lawrence Seaway was opened to vessels of 740 feet thereby permitting ocean going freighters access to the North American heartland. My first major experience with a salty was when returning from Toronto I locked up-bound in the Welland Canal with a Soviet freighter. (Note: "Seaway Welland, This is *Escape III*")

When I first started sailing on the Great Lakes in 1972, when crossing to Port Stanley, I would see as many as five or six freighters at night. In recent years, due the decline of steel production and the resulting emergence of the so-called "rust belt", I would sometimes see two and often no freighters when crossing.

Laker waiting to enter a Seaway lock.

Ore boats have the familiar configuration of the pilothouse at the bow and the engine power at the stern. Accompanying the pilothouse is a thin bowsprit projecting forward at the top of the bow. This bowsprit is to give the captain an awareness of the vessels relative orientation behind the pilothouse.

Most of the cargo in the 1970-80s was iron ore. The iron ore was removed from the ore boats by giant un-loaders called Huletts. During most of the 1900's Huletts were to be utilized in all the major steel producing centers of the Great Lakes. With the passing of time I watched ore boats begin to utilize self-loaders, which signaled the demise and eventual disappearance of the Huletts.

Most of the freighters on the Great Lakes are limited in length to 730 feet owing to the length of locks of the Welland Canal. These locks are 800 feet long. In the late 1970s, 1000 foot

Typical laker with self-loader

vessels began to be constructed. About twelve are presently being utilized. These vessels have access to Lake Superior via the Soo Locks, which are 1200 feet in length. These super lakers have the pilothouse in the stern and with their square shaped transoms (flat area at the stern) they appear more like large barges.

Great Lakes freighters are laid up usually sometime in November for the winter season depending on ice conditions on the lakes. Company owners wish to keep these costly and valuable vessels operating as long as they can. Lake Erie, the southern most and shallowest of the Great Lakes, often does not freeze over. I remember one year when Lake Erie did freeze over and some freighters became entrapped before they could safely winter in port. At the time I was flying regularly from Cleveland to Detroit over Lake Erie and could see the stranded vessels. They had to be supplied from the air until they could break free either by the icebreaker *Mackinaw* or the Spring thaw.

About as long as you can get in a Welland Canal lock.

Smaller commercial vessel in Welland Canal

Another Lake Erie observation from the air was the churning mud trailing behind freighters as they made their way in the shallower section of the southwest portion of the lake.

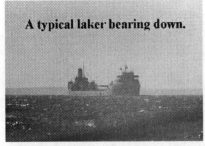
A typical laker bearing down.

Perusal of the many Great Lakes ship-wreck books reveal the stormy conditions of November as responsible for the multitude of tragedies the most noted and recent of which, was the *Edmund Fitzgerald.* The *Edmund Fitzgerald* went down in Lake Superior just off of Caribou Island in November 1975. In later years, I was to sail near the area where the *Edmund Fitzgerald* went down with 29 sailors.

Typical oreboat stern with more modern design.

The Great Lakes freighters have a long life since they are not subject to the corrosive effects of salt water. Many of the traditional style lakers have been utilized for more than fifty years and present the dominant configuration seen on the Great Lakes. Even the traditional design can esthetically be improved as exemplified by the *Edward L. Ryerson* that retains the traditional pilot house at the bow.

I was to eventually have additional observations of freighters in viewing what was reported to be the oldest coal burning freighter in Port Stanley; listening to anchor chains rattle as freighters let out anchors in the St. Marys River as a heavy fog suddenly set in; the "race" down the St. Marys River (as described later in *Journey to Michipicoten Island*) and the simple pleasure of observing the freighters on the lakes.

Port Stanley:

Port Stanley was to become my favorite port on the Great Lakes partially as a result of my initial warm contact with the Port Stanley Sailing Squadron. Through the years the *Mistress* was always welcomed and I developed several

A laker puts into Port Stanley

friends despite only getting there two or three times a year.

The Port Stanley Sailing Squadron is located on the east side of Kettle Creek just beyond the draw-bridge and adjacent to the business district. Across the creek lining the west bank are what look like bed mattresses. These were probably put in place as soft cement filled fabric containers and then hosed down to set the cement and prevent erosion.

The Port Stanley Sailing Squadron was made up of primarily middle-income citizens, which in addition to native Canadians, was partially comprised of several German and British immigrants. Most of these worked and lived in nearby St. Thomas, nine miles to the north or London twenty miles also to the north.

Typical Great Lakes commercial fishing boats along Kettle Creek

The river channel into Port Stanley opens to a small widening before coming to the draw-bridge. Several commercial fishing boats are docked within this opening.

Upstream, beyond the bridge, additional fishing boats are docked as well as the Port Stanley Sailing Squadron.

It seemed that each year stores in the small business district would change, as local entrepreneurs would try their hand at opening small shops. These generally catered to a small tourist business since Port Stanley is somewhat out of the way for pleasure boaters. Some preliminary attempts were made to establish a ferry service across the lake to Cleveland, but these never worked out. Selfishly, to my thinking, this limitation added to my own comprehension of personal charm to the "Port," as the locals often referred to it.

The most stable commercial activity in the central business area was a hardware store, a couple of small grocery establishments, a restaurant, small hotel, a liquor

Port Stanley business district as viewed from the bridge.

store and a bank, businesses that catered primarily to the local populace. This is not to say even the local establishments were constant. At one point the Clifton Hotel burned down, the bank closed, a local fisherman constructed a large building adjacent to the outer harbor housing a bar and possibly rooms to let.

Some locals converted an old building into the Kettle Creek Inn, a pleasant bed and breakfast with an evening dining area. Mr. Singer and I would regularly

The Kettle Creek Inn

frequent this establishment in the tiny three-stool bar, the adjacent restaurant, and garden patio.

Beyond the business area to the southwest is a large well-used beach with several bars. At one time a large pavilion was located adjacent to the beach with a 13,000 square foot swing and big band dance floor. Unfortunately, this renovated structure burned to the ground in on New Year's Eve of 1978-1979.

Across from the Port Stanley Sailing Squadron, along the west bank of Kettle Creek, the Port Stanley Terminal Rail Line runs between the old Port Stanley rail station adjacent the bridge to St. Thomas and points north. This line was once The London and Port Stanley Railway, which was eventually abandoned. A group of local residents and railroad aficionados purchased the abandoned right of way, made repairs, acquired some older diesel locomotives and rail passenger cars. After making one of the runs on the Port Stanley Terminal Rail Line, participants are encouraged to make comment in a guest book. One of the comments, for some reason that we still to this day find humorous, is "Truly Awesome."

In addition to frequenting the popular beach, the drinking and restaurant establishments, a trip on the "truly awesome" Port Stanley Terminal Rail Line, one further activity exists. That activity was attending the Port Stanley amateur theatre. I particularly remember one play written by one of the locals, produced and directed by one of the locals, staring some of the locals, the subject of which was about some of the fictitious local fisherman called, I believe, "For the Love of Perch". We always looked forward to attending these productions hoping they were not sold out as they often were.

One of my most memorable experiences at Port Stanley was suddenly being awakened one morning by a strange, yet familiar, sound. As I crawled into the cockpit of *Mistress* and looked over to the west bank, beyond the tracks of the Terminal Line, high on a hill were a couple of houses. On the front stoop of one of these houses a gentleman stood playing a bag-pipe as though it was his job to welcome a new day.

Vignettes of a Sailor

The Old Navy Guy:

Dick worked for me as a corporate real estate representative when I was a regional real estate manager for a major American company. Dick was about twenty years older than me. I was his boss due more to geographic circumstances than ability. I worked out of the headquarters office while Dick lived several hundred miles away.

Despite our age difference we became good friends and Dick liked to go sailing. I enjoyed having Dick aboard since he kept Mr. Singer and me entertained with countless numbers of war stories. During the Second World War Dick was a seaman (semaphore) in the U.S. Navy and traveled extensively in the Atlantic and Pacific Oceans.

One of the many stories he told was about a convoy run to Murmansk a port north of the Arctic circle. Murmansk, in the Soviet Union, was an Arctic supply port for the delivery of war materials by the Allies. In addition to contending with U-boats, convoys were attacked by air from Nazi occupied Norway. If they had been hit, as many were, survival time in the Arctic waters was a matter of minutes. In Murmansk, when a sailor got off his ship he was escorted by two soldiers to each of three bars where he was permitted two vodkas at each bar. He was then was directly escorted back to his ship. Forty years after the end of the war Dick was still bitter about their treatment by the Soviets (our "allies") and who could blame him.

Dick was in the Navy during most of the war and his exploits would in themselves be fodder for a book. Mr. Singer and I had the luxury of hearing about them along with occasional accompanying newspaper articles and Naval promotion letters he brought aboard the *Mistress*.

The first time I ran into a substantial fog was when Dick, his twelve year old son John, and my daughter Jennifer were making a trip to Port Stanley. Early one morning when we were about five miles out, an ore boat was departing as it blasted the appropriate fog signal. As many times as I had been into Port Stanley, rarely was there an ore boat in port. Great, I thought, why does an ore boat have to be coming out in this fog especially when I have two little kids aboard? The radar reflector* was hanging in the rigging and I was sure someone was monitoring the radar-scope especially since numerous commercial fishing boats work out of the port. The ore boat passed us and shortly thereafter we could feel its comparatively gentle wake despite never catching a glimpse of the passing vessel.

In the spring, when Mr. Singer and I would bring *Mistress* back to life, after winter storage, Dick usually managed to get from Cincinnati to Chagrin Lagoons. As with many boaters part of the ritual of getting a boat ready for haul-in involves the consumption of beer. Dick truly loved his beer and consequently fit in easily with this annual springtime ritual. Mr. Singer loved to pull Dick's chain and every year that Dick would show up Mr. Singer would say, "Hey, Dick are you back again to sand and paint your one square inch of the bottom?"

Despite having shipped out in both oceans of the war, Dick could care less about navigation. Upon sighting an ore

---

* Fiberglass sailboats even with a tall mast are stealth with regard to radar. To keep from being run down in limited visibility, a radar reflector must be utilized. A radar reflector is comprised of three metal dish-like panels interlocked with each other to form a series of corners. When a radar signal hits a radar reflector the radar signal bounces (reflects) off of one of the corners back to the vessel issuing the signal and shows up on the issuing vessel's radar screen. Hopefully, some one is manning the radar screen.

boat in the distance, Mr. Singer would tell him, "Aim directly for that boat," just to rattle Dick. Dick was a good sport as well as entertaining. He thoroughly enjoyed manning the helm, the comradeship, and drinking beer, especially drinking Canadian beer.

The Edbeau Incident:

One year in mid October I was anxious to get in one more crossing to Port Stanley. Mr. Singer could not go, but one of his friends, we jokingly called Edbeau, (Edson), could. The night before Edbeau and I consumed the demon rum and decided to crash where Edbeau lived with his parents at their nearby home.

Edbeau's parents were asleep and Edbeau insisted that I sleep in his bed while he slept on the living room couch. The next morning I was suddenly awakened when Edbeau's mother burst into the room, flicked on the overhead light and shouted, "Alright asshole, get up." As I pulled the cover down from my face, she said, "Oh my God, I'm sorry. Where's Ed?" The start of a new day.

Edbeau and I made our way to the *Mistress* and took off for Port Stanley. The sky was gray and the weather threatening, but by this time I was confident in my foul weather sailing abilities and the *Mistress.* We motored into the river and out into the lake. By now the weather was producing small tornados, clustered two or three at a time hanging within and on the edge of cloud formations.

Edbeau was now becoming increasingly sick. Strange, I thought since Edbeau had been sailing as crew on several racing boats as well as on Helmut's Tartan. Edbeau kept getting progressively sicker and finally said to me, "Cornell, I know how much you counted on going to Port Stanley this one last time, but if you turn around now, I'll think you're the greatest gentleman who ever lived. If you don't, I'll hate you for the rest of my life." Normally, I'd be adverse to turning around, especially now that we were about one-third the way across, but I began to worry. What if Edbeau was really sick from something such as appendicitis or some other malady?

As I turned *Mistress* to return to Chagrin Lagoons, Edbeau continued to hold his stomach and now had the dry heaves. About four hours later I tied up at my dock. The minute Edbeau stepped on to the dock, he instantly recovered. Mal de mer; it must be horrible.

"God Damn It! Why Didn't I Think of That?":

Helmut, on whose boat *Taboo* I had sailed to the islands and as a result decided to purchase the *Mistress,* and I had become friends as well as dock partners. Helmut, before coming to the United States had escaped from East Germany, smuggled himself back into East Germany and then escaped again with his wife Illsa.

Helmut was a fairly stern, semi-humorless individual, possibly because of his growing up in Nazi Germany and as a member of the Hitler Youth. Some incidents reflected his background. Helmut's daughter Connie and my daughter Jennifer as young teenagers occasionally hung out together. One time my wife went to pick them up after bowling. When she returned, she commented on how with the teenager style at the time (straight hair and wire rim glasses) all the kids looked like they were in uniform. In his thick German accent Helmut said, "What is wrong with children being in uniform?" Another time when Helmut and I were sailing in a storm at night I jokingly asked, "Helmut, have you ever been this frightened before?" Helmut's response was, "Yaa, when I was in a building that was bombed during the war."

Helmut had become very successful with a small machine shop. I had watched Helmut equip *Taboo* with certain items with, which I also wanted to equip *Mistress.*

One of these items was a second set of winches, which had to be mounted on a pad to be placed on the coaming in order to clear the lifelines. Helmut was ordering these pads and asked if I also wanted pads. I answered affirmatively. If Helmut was putting additional winches on *Taboo,* I also had to have them on the *Mistress.*

There was a problem in mounting the pads. The surface on which they were to be mounted was a compound surface, i.e. there were two flat surfaces with different angles. Having a machine shop and instruments Helmut was able to machine and transfer these angles to the pads so that the pads would sit perfectly onto the compound surface. Helmut would often say, "God damn it, how does anybody own a boat without owning a machine shop?" Helmut was now waiting for me to come to him to request that he prepare my pads for mounting.

One day I brought the pads up on deck, placed one on the uneven surface. Helmut was watching attentively expecting me to ask for assistance. I then marked the area where the pad would be mounted, pulled out an electric drill with a grinder and ever so slightly ground down the fiberglass surface until the flat surface of the pad fit comfortably on to the fiberglass.

Helmut shook his head and said, "God damn it! Why didn't I think of that?" Being the unkind and nasty guy that I am, I just said, "Helmut, why do you think we won the war?" Despite this ungentlemanly response, Helmut and I remained friends for many years to come.

A Near Death Experience:

Mr. Singer and I have been in comparatively dangerous circumstances including lightening hitting the water around us, torrential rain storms, water spouts, dense fog, and several on shore altercations. Most of these occurred with regularity and seldom stood out as particularly memorable incidents.

It's the unexpected, which stands out as being memorable. One evening, Mr. Singer and I were making our way back to *Mistress* after favoring numerous beach area and business district refreshment establishments. It was dark as we turned from the well-lit roadway on to the short street, which led to the Port Stanley Sailing Squadron clubhouse. As usual Mr. Singer and I were discussing subjects of great importance, if only to us.

As we walked along I asked, "Well, what d'ya think?" No response. I looked around. No Mr. Singer. Then I heard a moan. Mr. Singer had fallen into an unmarked manhole excavation. I looked down into the manhole and there was Mr. Singer spread out at the bottom between several steel rebars projecting upward from the base of the hole. It was miraculous how Mr. Singer had fallen into the hole without impaling himself. I guess it was because God didn't want me to have to sail back to Chagrin single-handed.

I pulled Mr. Singer out and we brushed the dirt off him. "God damn it! Why didn't those *#@%&* fence off the hole or at least cover it." Nearby, lay a large sheet of plywood, perhaps originally covering the hole. Did someone forget to cover it after work or did some kids move it?

We pulled the plywood sheet over the hole. "Let's get back out on the water where at least it's safe," grumbled Mr. Singer.

Won in a Card Game:

The best example of ignorance being dangerously bliss was when one year we had crossed Lake Erie to Port Stanley, Ontario. We were heading back to the *Mistress* from a swim on the beach when a passing fellow with a young lady asked, "Hey man, where can we get some beer?" I told him, "There's a small store just around the corner. Where are you guys from?" "Oh, we just crossed the lake from the Chagrin River at Eastlake, Ohio." "We're from Eastlake also. Where's your boat?" I asked. Anxious to be off for his beer he said, "My buddy is cruising around in the river by the bridge until I get back with the beer." I told Mr. Singer, "Let's go check this out."

When we got to the bridge, there circling around in the river was about a 16 foot open boat complete with a guy, his wife, an outboard engine and a cracked windshield. This was one of those early fiber-glass boats complete with 1950s automobile styled tail fins.

I called out, "Hey, come over here." He was, to say the least, reluctant until I yelled over, "We just talked to your buddy who said you were from Chagrin. We're also from Chagrin." Slowly he pulled toward the edge of the creek and tossed some old clothes-lines. "You guys came across in that?" I asked. "Yeah, I always wanted to come across and I won this boat in a card game last night."

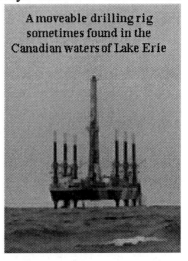

A moveable drilling rig sometimes found in the Canadian waters of Lake Erie

"Well why did you come to Port Stanley, which is 70 miles from Chagrin rather than Rondeau which is only about 50 miles?" He responded, "We were heading for Rondeau, but we couldn't find it." "Well how did you find Port Stanley?" queried Mr. Singer. "We came across a drilling rig*

---

* The Canadians, a very environment friendly people, have been drilling and capping gas wells on Lake Erie for several years. Wonder why they can do it and not the United States? These rigs are moved around in the Canadian waters. When in the desired position, adjustable stanchions are lowered to the lake bed and the rig is stationary. Fortunately, they are lit by bright fluorescent lights at night.

and asked them to point us to the nearest port and here we are."

Just then I noticed a cheap automobile compass mounted on the cracked windshield. This was shocking enough, but I also saw, next to the compass on the dashboard a packet containing several tools. "Take those tools away from the compass. Don't you know how ferrous-metal affects a compass?" He looked at me blankly and said, "Ferrous-metal?"

I then noticed he had a red fuel can hooked to the outboard. "How much fuel did you have remaining when you arrived?" "About a quarter of a tank." I warned him, "The wind has been blowing out of the south all day which helped you along. Now you'll be heading right into the wind. You'll probably run out of fuel." By now he was getting perturbed as well as embarrassed in front of his wife and looked up at us and said in a truly macho manner, "Look, I can take care of myself as well as my wife."

Just then, his buddy and girl friend returned, climbed aboard and headed down the river, after which Mr. Singer and I headed back to the *Mistress* both knowing that they would not make it, or at least not that day.

About a half hour later as we were tipping a few brews in the cockpit of the *Mistress* the macho boys came back up the river and as they passed yelled out, "Is there a hotel in this town?" "Yeah, you can probably get rooms at the Clifton Hotel."

That Saturday night we saw the macho boys and girls at the weekly Clifton Hotel dance oblivious of their predicament. The next morning we departed for home and never heard from or about the macho gang again. Ignorance is not only bliss, but also dangerous.

The Traditionalist:

Mr. Singer and I were once again in the Welland Canal returning from Toronto. Several pleasure boats were to be clustered together when passing through each lock. Every now and then boat manufacturers, particularly manufacturers of sailboats, would introduce a boat design that would feed off of a sail boater's nostalgia. These vessels would incorporate some of the traits of older sailboat designs.

One of these sailboats of an older design was included in the group that was to transit the canal. The owner, in his attempt to blend with his traditional boat, dressed the part complete with suspender held denim trousers, an old flannel shirt and a traditional captains hat much like that worn by Wolf Larson (Edward G. Robinson) in the 1941 movie "The Sea Wolf". Of course to complete the image the traditionalist had to have a beard and smoke a pipe while telling his adventurous sea stories to his ship-mate.

After passing through the first up-bound seven locks, the canal becomes a lockless stretch of seventeen miles before reaching the final lock number eight. Within this seventeen-mile stretch the traditionalist moved out in front of and about one hundred yards away from the cluster of boats. While still yakking to his ship-mate, he elected to proceed down the middle of the canal as the cluster stayed to the right side of the canal. Soon, in the distance, a down-bound ore boat appeared coming toward us. Closer and closer came the ore boat. The traditionalist continued making his merry way down the center of the canal. Closer and closer came the ore boat. Mr. Singer and I became alarmed, as the traditionalist was apparently unaware of the approaching potential catastrophic situation. Fortunately, at what seemed to be the last minute, the traditionalist looked forward and, with great dismay, instantly turned his boat ninety degrees to starboard and missed having an impending disaster.

As we continued, I said to Mr. Singer, "I'd sure like to hear what he would have to say at the end of the canal." Mr. Singer, with his ability to make a humorous comment in any situation simply said. "Yeah, but I'd sure rather see his underwear."

When we got to the end of the canal at Port Colborne, the traditionalist, rather than embarrassingly face other boaters continued on his way. I never did get to hear what the traditionalist had to say and Mr. Singer never did get to check his underwear.

How The *Damn Thing* Got It's Name:

I had secured a light weight two-man dinghy that we towed when traveling off-shore. On a weekend journey across Lake Erie to Port Stanley Mr. Singer and I were spending a quiet relaxing afternoon at the Port Stanley Sailing Squadron. As we sat in the cockpit of the Mistress a young lady came laboriously rowing toward a nearby dock.

The *Damn Thing*

As she crashed the bow of the dinghy onto the dock, she threw a line across the dock, grabbed the dock, pulled the dinghy alongside and, with great difficulty, crawled onto the dock. Once on the dock, she grabbed the line and yelled to some boaters at a nearby marina, "How the hell do you tie up the damn thing?" One of the boaters from the marina ran over to the dock and assisted the damsel in distress in tying up the damn thing.

Mr. Singer and I were quite amused at watching this display and then it came to me. "Mr. Singer, I just thought of a name for the dinghy." "What's that?" came the response with tears from laughter in his eyes." *Damn Thing,* we'll call the dinghy the *Damn Thing.* Just think, what an appropriate name. "Get into the *Damn Thing;* Tie off the *Damn Thing;* Should we take the *Damn Thing* along?" Henceforth, the dinghy would be referred to as the *Damn Thing.*

Seven Days to Nowhere

During the late 1960's several sailors were to make news with tremendous exploits. One of these was that of Robert Manry. Manry was a copy editor at the Plain Dealer, a Cleveland newspaper. In the summer of 1965, Manry completed a 78-day sail from Falmouth, Massachusetts to Falmouth, England. The historic nature of Manry's voyage was the Atlantic crossing was completed in a 13.5-foot boat, the smallest known vessel ever to cross the Atlantic. The small wooden sailboat, which Manry named *Tinkerbell.*, was altered by Manry. He modified the cockpit and added a small cabin. As a result of this achievement, Manry became a celebrated world figure, particularly in Cleveland where his *Tinkerbelle* is now kept as an exhibit at the Western Reserve Historical Society in Cleveland.

In 1967, Francis Chichester was knighted for sailing around the world with one stop at Sydney, Australia. I remember authorities were considering preventing Chichester from completing his voyage across the vast Pacific, rounding Cape Horn, and home to England. Fortunately, no one interfered with him. The world was truly enthralled with the accomplishment of this sixty-seven year old man.

The following year Robin Knox Johnston circumnavigated the globe in the first solo non stop race. I could never hope to match or even come close to these exploits, but I mention them since they were inspirational. As a sailor, these almost unbelievable accomplishments started me thinking, what would it be like to spend a period of time, albeit comparatively short, aboard the *Mistress*? Up until this time I had only sailed two days without docking or anchoring. How would I feel after seven days of continuous sailing? There was only one way to find out. Since Lake Erie is relatively crowded with commercial shipping and at this time I did not have a self-steering device, to achieve this objective, I would have to have a sailing companion.

"Mr. Singer, What do you think about sailing for seven days non stop?" I figured Mr. Singer would think I had lost it. "Yeah! That would be interesting. Let's do it. We can sail in any direction, depending only on the wind." While this would not begin to compare with the circumnavigators, we just wanted to see what our psychological reaction would be to stay on the water for longer than an occasional one or two day trip.

Our considerations were three-fold. First, neither of us could take longer than a week from our jobs; second, there was a considerable amount of shipping traffic, which would necessitate a continual watch; and third, we did not have an automatic steering device. Fortunately, with proper sail trim, and a break on the helm, occasionally we would be able to sail for a few hours without manning the helm. This could only occur if the wind was steady in intensity and direction. This condition is rarely found on Lake Erie or any of the Great Lakes.

We stocked up on canned foods, breakfast pastries, some hardboiled eggs, various non-perishable food packets and bags and blocks of ice. (The *Mistress* did not yet have refrigeration) Soon after, we cast off at 0730 under an overcast sky and set a course for Port Stanley, Ontario. The wind was out of the southwest and the sea was running eight to fourteen feet. Later it began to rain, which had the effect of calming the sea to about four feet. At 1730 (the next day) Port Stanley was spotted in hazy visibility.

Port Stanley is a deep-water port with buoys marking the channel into the port fed by Kettle Creek. Mr. Singer has always called these buoys "rockets" since they were narrow and shaped like rockets. Psychologically, the most trying conflict came early in the venture. Initially, after the sail across the lake, to continue our objective we circled one of the channel buoys leading into port. It was difficult not to enter the harbor and visit with the many friends I had made over the last six years. We circled the buoy and off we went toward Erie, Pennsylvania.

The Eastern End:

As we made our way toward Erie the wind increased to twenty-plus knots and was swinging to the west. On this course we passed the deepest point, 210 feet, of Lake Erie between Erie, Pennsylvania and Long Point Peninsula.[*] By 0300 the lights of Erie were spotted. When just off shore at 0630, we turned northward and a course was set for the east end of Long Point. At this point our first emergency occurred. One of the pad-eye bolts on the bottom of the boom came out. This pad-eye held one end of the main sheet.[**] The mainsheet threaded through several blocks and back to the cockpit. It was imperative that this be repaired immediately.

The first thing to be done was to ease the main sheet to take the pressure off the pad-eye before the second bolt pulled out. Earlier Mr. Singer had assisted me in placing pad eyes on the mast and left the thread cutting equipment (taps) on board. Mr. Singer used the tool to rethread where the bolt had come out and secured the pad-eye with a new bolt. This repair has lasted to this day. More importantly, I learned that there can never be too many tools aboard along with an array of nuts, bolts, and cotter pins.

By 1100 we passed the east end of Log Point and headed north, northwest for a mid channel buoy located

---

[*] Lake Erie, by far, is the shallowest of the Great Lakes. The other four lakes are considerably deeper ranging from 750 feet (Lake Huron) to 1333 feet (Lake Superior).

[**] The mainsheet controls the boom and thus, the main sail.

approximately five miles off the Ontario shore. After rounding the mid channel buoy at 1300, course was set for Dunkirk, New York. The wind was from the northwest and the sky a clear bright blue. "Hey Corn, Think we should try the whisker pole,* the wind is moving directly behind us?" The whisker pole was a new addition to the *Mistress* and neither of us quite knew how to set it. Mr. Singer went forward on the deck. Eventually he managed to get the whisker pole positioned. We enjoyed the ride for several hours as the sky became overcast. The wind was increasing to above forty knots and the waves were building. As I looked behind the rolling waves were towering and looked like they would engulf the *Mistress.* As each wave rolled under us, the *Mistress*'s stern would rise. Finally, I told Mr. Singer, "Better get the pole down." By this time we were achieving speeds of twelve knots as we slid down each massive wave.

As Mr. Singer struggled on the heaving foredeck he was able to unhook the whisker pole. When he did so, the pole accidentally dipped into the water and the end of the pole broke. Mr. Singer managed to get the pole secured and we were forced to slightly change our course. I was more interested in dealing with the sea and wind condition, which by this time was shifting to the southwest. By 2000 the power company stacks at Dunkirk, New York were spotted to the southwest and the wind subsided as the sea condition began to flatten. As a result of the stormy condition, we were northeast of Dunkirk, nearer to Silver Creek, New York.

We began tacking westward and by 2300 we were past Dunkirk. We then sailed in a westerly direction as the wind

---

* A whisker pole is a pole attached to the vessel. In the case of the *Mistress* to a pad-eye on the mast. The pole can be extended and attached to the outer base (foot) corner of the sail (clew). This holds the sail out in order to catch more wind when sailing downwind (wing & wing).

was minimal out of the southwest and the sky was clearing. We were practically becalmed as we again slowly crossed the shipping lanes. So what if we were practically becalmed? The objective was to stay on the water for seven days rather than get somewhere. Besides, this respite in weather gave us a welcome chance to bathe. Bathing on the *Mistress* involved tossing a bucket attached to a lanyard overboard, filling it with lake water, going to the foredeck, scrubbing up and dumping buckets of cool lake water atop ourselves. Kind of cold, but effective enough that Mr. Singer and I could stand to be within smelling distance of each other.

By 0500 the wind had increased to 16 knots. We were soon sailing in a west, northwest direction. The wind was constant. Perfect for setting sail and utilizing the wheelbreak. In this fashion *Mistress* was able to maintain an unmanned course, with no sail adjustment, for over three and one-half hours. During a portion of this period, I ran the engine to charge the batteries.

By 2100 we were paralleling the north shore off Long Point peninsula. As we got closer to Port Stanley we spotted two brightly lit Canadian drilling rigs located to the southeast of Port Stanley. By 0500 we were again rounding one of the "rocket" buoys outside Port Stanley for the second time and headed back to the Chagrin River area. Throughout a bright clear day the wind was light and the lake surface flat. Crossing the paths of a few ore boats, we sailed until 2000 at which time we rounded a racing buoy outside the Chagrin River area and headed for the Pelee Passage.

The Western End:

Slowly the wind was steadily increasing. "Mr. Singer, I think were going to reduce sail." Surprised, Mr. Singer asked, "Why would we do that? The weather's not threatening." "I just have a feeling, the way this wind is building, let's get ready. It's easier to reef* now rather than later if the wind builds tonight. Besides we can always shake out the reef if the wind doesn't increase."

As we set a course almost due west for the Pelee Passage the wind increased out of the north in excess of 25 knots. We were relatively close to Cleveland and were able to observe numerous fireworks displays in various communities along the south shore. It was July 4th. Throughout the night and early morning a strong wind held. We were able to maintain an average speed of seven knots while ensconced alternately between the cockpit and cabin. "Hey, Mr. Singer, want some beef stew?" Amazing how good canned beef stew can taste at 0100.

At 0530 we passed through the Pelee Passage noting a couple of down bound freighters. Running in a northwest-southeast direction between Point Pelee, Ontario and Pelee Island, transit through the Pelee Passage is comparatively simple for small pleasure and fishing craft. For deep draft Great Lakes freighters it is a narrow passage, which funnels traffic between eastern and western Lake Erie. Pelee Point is a narrow peninsula which projects southward from the Canadian shore and is the southern most point of the Canadian mainland. The area was made into a national park in 1918 partially because of being a part of a bird and butterfly migration route. Over 350 bird species have been spotted in the park.

---

* Reefing is when the sail area is reduced by partially lowering a sail and tying the bottom portion to the boom. As mentioned previously *Escape III* had roller reefing wherein the sail was wrapped around the boom. Reefing points are found in the form of small tie lines in the sail, which are used to tie the sail to the boom. The main sail on *Mistress* had two settings for reefing. I found that, due to the frequency and intensity of squalls on the Great Lakes, it was necessary to utilize a full or maximum reef. A partial reef would more likely be used on oceans, where weather usually has a tendency to develop over a longer period of time.

Pelee Island, the largest of the Lake Erie islands, is located to the southwest of the passage. At less than 16 square miles Pelee Island supports a permanent population of approximately 250. In the past the island had primarily a viniculture base, but now had a mixed agriculture base. One of the major characteristics of the island populace, as with all the area islands, is its wintertime isolation interrupted only by occasional air service.

As daylight intensified into a clear blue sky the wind began to moderate. At 0800 we rounded the buoy, which marks Colchester Reef. Colchester Reef is a shallow area (10 feet deep) about four miles south of the Canadian Shore, a potentially dangerous impediment to deep draft vessels making their way from the Pelee Passage to the mouth of the Detroit River. "Corn, where do ya think we should head for now?" "Well Mr. Singer, the wind is shifting to the northwest. I'm gonna check the chart to see where a southwest course might take us. In the meantime let's shake out that reef and have some breakfast."

One of the nice things about how we were sailing was we didn't have to deal with a contrary wind. We could set a course wherever the wind might take us. "It looks like we can make Middle Sister Island about ten miles to the southwest." The ten mile span between Colchester Reef and Middle Sister Island defines the area through which commercial freighters pass in making their way between the Pelee Passage and the mouth of the Detroit River. The Colchester Reef at night is identified by a flashing red light. Middle Sister Island is marked with a flashing green light. The color of these lights follow a general navigation rule, "red right, returning". Returning is generally traveling up stream or in the case of Lake Erie against the general flow of water. Thus, in traveling from Pelee Passage to the mouth of the Detroit River (against the general flow) the light on Colchester Reef is red.

After passing Middle Sister Island we continued in a southwest direction toward West Sister Island another ten miles to the southwest. Later in the day we reached West Sister Island. We sat becalmed the remainder of the day and well into the next morning, twelve hours with barely a breath of wind. Strange how we always found something to do particularly during these calm periods; cooking, cleaning up below, scrubbing the deck and cockpit, waxing the fiberglass, cleaning and oiling the teak.

We did have endless hours of conversation about numerous subjects many of which we knew nothing. Funny how one can always have an opinion about most things. Mr. Singer, as I had mentioned, had an extremely broad knowledge of science, math and mechanics. My limited knowledge was in history, geography, and the business world. This dichotomy of knowledge helped us keep each other entertained for hours.

We did have one other form of entertainment, the commercial radio. Besides the normal music programs, a Detroit station had two guys on in the morning. I don't remember their names, but they were heavily involved in little humorous skits involving what they called the "Whoa Boys", and the "Sam Sakowitz Department Store" where you could get automotive service on the fifth floor. Sam had a wife named Beau and they had named their son Sambeau. Goofy stuff, but hilarious when you're out of touch for a couple of days. As can be noted, it sure didn't take much to keep us entertained. Mr. Singer and I still occasionally joke about the "Whoa Boys" and the "Sam Sakowitz Department Store" thirty years later.

When the wind began to come alive it was coming out of the west. We now elected to sail southeast through the South Passage approximately seventeen miles to the southeast. The South Passage separates the mainland from the group of Lake Erie islands, specifically South Bass Island and Kellys Island.

Passing South Bass Island was reminiscent of passing Port Stanley earlier in the voyage. I had been to South Bass Island a few years earlier in my former vessel, *Escape III*. The town of Put-in-Bay, fed by ferries from the mainland and yachtsmen, is the summertime tourist-party center of all the islands. The main street of Put-in-Bay faces a bay filled with pleasure boats and the mainland ferry. The main street is also lined with tourist oriented shops, restaurants, and saloons. One of these saloons is the Beer Barrel Saloon, which is reported to be the third longest bar in the world. One of the major attractions (other than the saloons) of South Bass Island is the Perry's Victory and International Peace Memorial. This 317 foot Doric column commemorates Perry's naval victory on Lake Erie over the British during the War of 1812. ("Don't give up the ship.") The monument also commemorates the longest unfortified border in the world.

Kellys Island is the largest of the American islands. While Kellys Island has two attractions, the glacial grooves and Native American pictographs, tourism was not a major economic activity on the island, especially when compared to Put-in-Bay.

By 0600 we had traversed the South Passage and were three miles east of the Marblehead Light. The Marblehead Light marks the eastern most extension of the northern peninsula that forms Sandusky Bay. Again it was time to confer as to what direction we should take. "We could just sail around the island area," suggested Mr. Singer. I countered with "Naw, I'd like to get back into open water." The wind was out of the northwest and we finally settled on heading for Rondeau Harbour about 45 miles to the northeast.

Twenty-two hours later the lights at Rondeau Harbour were spotted. We finally approached the channel entrance to Rondeau Harbour at 0900. This entrance is marked by a light perched atop a white concrete pyramid shaped structure. Other than when we were becalmed, this was the slowest (27 hours) segment of our journey. One of the benefits of this slow quiet progression was again we did not have to man the helm every moment when under way. Even though one of us had to be on watch, the person on watch could stretch out on the aft seat behind the helm and doze while setting an alarm clock for 1/2 hour or 1/4 hour if in the shipping lanes. This technique, which we used in many future excursions could only be applied, as mentioned previously, on open water with good visibility, a steady wind and non-stormy conditions.

Unlike most of our experiences in the eastern portion of the lake, the sky was clear and the surface relatively calm. The wind was now out of the southwest shifting to the northwest and then north. We welcomed the darkness since the sun had been blazing hot. We continued northeast paralleling the Ontario shore and once again headed for Port Stanley about another 50 miles distant.

One of the advantages of sailing ten or fifteen miles off shore with the wind coming off shore is that the waves do not have a long distance to build. A fairly strong wind blowing over a long distance (fetch) can substantially increase the height of waves.

As we got closer Port Stanley the wind was shifting to out of the north and northeast on the nose. Even though we were primarily sailing to take best advantage of the wind, it was time to run the engine and recharge the batteries again. As a result, it was decided to continue under power on a northeast course.

We reached the "rockets", as Mr. Singer called them, off Port Stanley, late in the afternoon. By this time the wind had died and again we were becalmed. Again we took up the usual maintenance items, but also repairing an air vent to the head.

As darkness approached we once again turned toward Chagrin seventy miles to the south. By this time the lightened wind had shifted further from northeast to the east. "Mr. Singer, I think we had better go under power. I don't think we're going to get much wind and we both have to go to work on Monday." Reluctantly, Mr. Singer agreed and we continued under power. We docked at the same dock from which we had departed seven days, one and one half hours previously and traversed over seven hundred miles.

During this journey we ran into the weather extremes provided by Lake Erie, made repairs while under way, conversed endlessly, relaxed, cleaned, read, and sunned ourselves. In our run to both ends of the lake we crossed the shipping lanes nine times, silently glided through groups of hundreds of sport fishing boats and spotted numerous tow boats, ore boats and salties. I thought at the end of such an experience I would be ready for a break from sailing. Instead, I was ready to continue and really didn't care if I concluded this sail. Unfortunately, making a living won out.

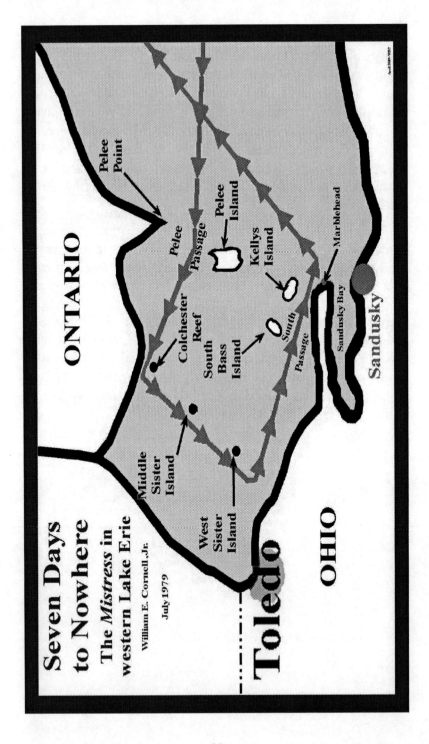

Seven Days
to Nowhere

The *Mistress* in
western Lake Erie

William E. Cornell ,Jr.

July 1979

ONTARIO

OHIO

Toledo

Sandusky

Pelee
Point

Pelee
Passage

Pelee
Island

Kellys
Island

Marblehead

Sandusky Bay

Colchester
Reef

South
Bass
Island

South
Passage

Middle
Sister
Island

West
Sister
Island

98

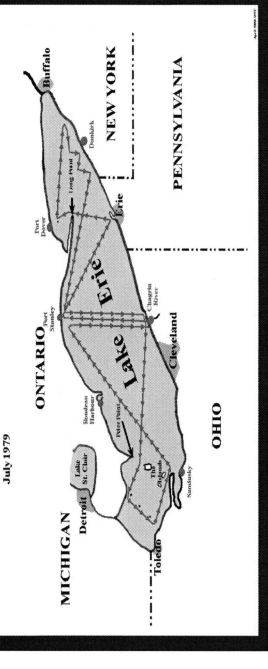

Seven Days to Nowhere

The *Mistress* sails Lake Erie for seven days

William E. Cornell, Jr.

July 1979

Voyage to Michipicoten Island

Most people desire to have an adventure or adventures as a part of their lives. While most of us must succumb to the everyday requirements of raising a family, making a living, and paying bills, our mundane existence is occasionally punctuated by a tragedy or some sort of crises. If we're lucky, the mundane existence can be punctuated by an adventure of our own making, very often a vacation or pursuit of a hobby. In my particular instance, I was able to combine limited vacation times with sailing.

As an avid reader of the sailing adventures of others, it was again time to make my own sailing adventure, within the confines of an all too limited vacation period.

Cruising sailors peruse charts and imagine sailing off to distant ports. I don't know exactly when, (maybe one day while day dreaming at work) but at some time I decided it was time for a long cruise. As mentioned previously, I had sailed across and around Lake Erie, made the trip through the Welland Canal on to Lake Ontario to Toronto, Canada. Now it was time for something more challenging. One evening I went home and began to look over an old chart of the Great Lakes issued (like gas stations used to do with state highway maps) by oil companies. Let's see, I thought, how far can I go by sail and return in two weeks? Don't forget, hopefully, I would still have a job and a family to take care off.

Detroit? No, not far enough. Lake Huron, the Georgian Bay, Sault St. Marie near the entrance to Lake Superior, the greatest of the Great Lakes? Then it struck me. A small, about 15 miles by 5 miles, island situated 10 miles south of the north shore of Ontario and about 105 miles northwest of where Lake Superior flows into the St. Marys River. Michipicoten Island. That's it. I couldn't pronounce it, but I knew I wanted to go there.

When I proposed the thought of sailing off to Michipicoten Island and back in two weeks, Mr. Singer did not think twice and agreed that this would be challenging adventure, one of which he would naturally wish to be involved.

Getting Ready:

I knew I had a vessel, which I was confident could sail us, in reasonable comfort and safety to distant Michipicoten. I had been able to secure charts for Lakes Erie, Ontario, Huron, and St. Clair. I could have sent for the Lake Superior charts, but at the time, I was traveling extensively for business and felt that surely I would be able to secure the necessary Lake Superior charts in Detroit or Chicago. Wrong, at least if available, I couldn't find them at the time.

As we prepared to depart, I assured Mr. Singer and probably myself, "Don't worry. We'll find a port that has Lake Superior charts somewhere along the way."

The only electronic navigation system I had at the time was an RDF (radio direction finder). The RDF could pick up navigation signals (Morse code) and commercial radio stations. By tuning in a signal or commercial station one could dial a ferrite antenna mounted on a compass rose and determine a line of position. That is, a line on a chart drawn from the position of the signal to the position of the vessel. Theoretically, you were located somewhere along that line. If you could do the same for a second signal, where the line of the second signal crossed the line of the first signal, your estimated position would be established. The trouble with using a commercial radio station was that you had to know and be able to plot on a chart the exact location of the broadcasting antenna.

Often in addition to triangulating a position, the RDF was used to find a signal such as one sent from the port of destination, if an RDF signal was available at that port. Once determined, you could then head in that direction. A fairly crude form of navigation by today's standard, but it worked. *

At about this time, a navigation system called LORAN was beginning to be used on pleasure boats. Developed during World War II, LORAN utilized land based signals which when received could determine a position. Mr. Singer suggested the possibility of getting a LORAN receiver before our journey. I thought about this for a millisecond and rejected the idea. No, we needed to hone our skills in the art of piloting** a vessel. Besides, I didn't think I could afford such a luxury at the time.

Piloting is a comparatively simple process if one is aware of a few basic principles. I am amazed at the number of people that often venture into one of the most dangerous bodies of water in the world with no comprehension of the dangers resulting from the weather, unfound vessels, poor equipment, or a lack of knowledge of how to handle a boat or navigate.

---

* Japanese used Honolulu commercial radio stations to assist in making their way to home in on Pearl Harbor in 1941. Also, the British Navy was able to pinpoint the location of the Bismarck by radio direction signals when the Bismarck radioed Berlin for instructions.

** Piloting is when navigating, a vessel's position is determined by combining compass direction with time, speed, and relative bearings of identifiable landmarks and buoys. When there are no land marks or buoys visible an estimated position is determined by using speed. time and distance. An estimated position can be determined if calculations commence from a known or previously estimated position and depends on the accuracy of the instruments.

Another possible piece of equipment that would have been helpful would be an auto-helm, which is a device designed to keep a vessel on course without constantly controlling or monitoring the helm. After all, we planned to sail comparatively long distances night and day. An automatic steering device would permit us to sail for long periods of time with out constantly manning the helm. This was not a significant problem particularly since there would be two of us aboard. Also, the *Mistress* had a brake on the binnacle. When tightened, the brake locked the rudder. Thus, when locked and sails properly trimmed, one did not have to constantly man the helm. Any shift in the wind, either the brake would have to be released, or the sails reset or both before the brake could again be reapplied. This permitted a respite from constantly manning the helm. While less so in recent years, at this time (1980) the Great Lakes had considerable traffic so one had to be vigilant in maintaining a lookout.

As we had done when sailing as mentioned in *Seven Days to Nowhere,* while one of us was below sleeping, the other on watch would set an alarm for 1/2 hour or 1/4 hour if in the shipping lanes. This technique could only be used on open water with good visibility. We would not have to man the helm every moment when under way.

Besides, wasn't Joshua Slocum* able to cross the Atlantic twice and circle the globe without an auto helm?

---

* Many boaters, particularly sailors, know of or have read Slocum's "Sailing Alone Around the World". Slocum was a professional seagoing owner/captain who made numerous commercial sailing voyages around the world in the late 1800's. As steam powered vessels began to dominate commercial shipping and sailing vessels were converted to barges, Slocum's skills as a sailing captain were no longer in demand. Given an old derelict, slowly rotting on shore, 36-foot sailing vessel called the *Spray,* Slocum proceeded to rebuild the *Spray* and sail into history as the first around the world solo sailor.

As mentioned previously, I had secured a light-weight two-man dinghy, the *Damn Thing* that we towed when traveling off-shore. We planned to tow the *Damn Thing* as we journeyed north.

We now felt ready to commence, not what would be a significant sailing expedition, but what to us was to be a significant sailing adventure.

While involved in weekend preparations for the voyage we both had the requirement of maintaining a job during the week. During a business trip to the Detroit area, I was telling a business associate about the proposed trip to Michipicoten. Chris, over the years, had become a good friend. Chris lamented, "Wish I could go along." "Why don't you?" I asked. Chris owned and managed several properties in the Pontiac, MI area and just couldn't take the time. "Why don't you fly down to Cleveland, start out the trip for a couple of days and we'll drop you off some place in Michigan?" Chris thought for a minute and said, "O.K., when should I fly to Cleveland?"

The Start:

I picked Chris up at the Cleveland airport after his brief twenty-minute flight from Detroit and made our way to the *Mistress*. Mr. Singer was already aboard finalizing and packing away things for our departure. We departed Chagrin Lagoons at 4:30 a.m. on a west, northwest, (300 degrees) course once again bound for the Pelee Passage approximately sixty miles distant.

At this time, the mouth of the Chagrin River had developed an underwater sand bank extending out into the lake from the east bank of the river. Occasional weekend fishermen would come down the river and seeing open water to the north and northeast, would open-up their usually small outboard powered fishing vessel and immediately run aground. Fear of this invisible sand bank prevented many yachtsmen from entering the Chagrin River.

Extending from the west bank was, and is, a steel pile driven wall with comparatively deep water at the end. When we departed, we took a sharp turn to port at the end of the wall and took our west, northwest, course bound for the Pelee Passage.

Lake Erie was like a mill-pond, flat with no wind. We plugged along under power for over eight hours before any wind developed. Finally, a little past noon a very light wind came out of the east and we were able to shut down the engine and go under sail. Sailors know the joy of the silence after the monotonous droning of an engine for several hours. Ah, the silence. We were, albeit slow, thoroughly enjoying the change.

It seemed that this would be a pretty uneventful afternoon. Occasionally, we'd interrupt reading or dozing, plot a position on the chart, while keeping a lookout for other vessels heading to or coming from the Pelee Passage. The silence was broken only by the radio and the gentle sound of water on the hull.

At 17:30 we spotted the "B" bell buoy. This is a buoy that clangs due to rocking from wave action. It also marks the international boundary of Canada and the United States.

Ore boats passing in the Pelee Passage

The nice thing about spotting this buoy was that it confirmed our position on the chart and confirmed our heading to the Pelee Passage. We transited the passage and passed through with a barge and ore boats at 1930. The wind was still light and it looked like we would have a quiet, if not slow passage to the mouth of the Detroit River.

Sometime during the wee hours of the morning an unusual foreign sound was heard. "Peeeng". "What the hell was that?" I asked Mr. Singer. "Damned if I know," came the response. "Quiet, listen." Another "peeeng" was heard, but this time it was determined that it came from below in the cabin.

"Take the helm Mr. Singer, standby Chris, I'm going below." I made my way down the companionway into the darkened cabin. When underway, interior cabin lights were kept off for two reasons. First, and most importantly, lights interfered with night vision. Secondly, a sailboat when, under sail, has a limited amount of battery power that should be preserved.

I listened for another "peeeng". Silence. I sat down and waited. Then again, "peeeng". "You see anything?" shouted Mr. Singer. "Yeah, sounds like its coming from the ice box." Again, I waited for another "peeeng" Sure enough, the sound was emanating from the icebox. I switched on a cabin light and opened the icebox to look inside. "See anything?" yelled Mr. Singer. "I sure do," I said. As I climbed into the cockpit, I handed Mr. Singer a frozen, distorted can of beer. The top of the can was rounded and looked ready to explode.

Mr. Singer, in preparation for the voyage had packed the icebox with, not only beer, but also several pounds of dry ice. Not only were the cans distorted, but also the water content inside was frozen. You can imagine what was left inside. The advantage was that all you had to do was pop the top and quickly hold the can up to your mouth while the content flowed out under the pressure of being frozen. It was reassuring to know that the "peeeng" was nothing more than what were to become known as "beersicles".

We continued westerly toward the mouth of the Detroit River under light air. The surface was flat and it became hazy. About 0600 we spotted the channel buoys leading to the entrance to the Detroit River and finally entered the river about 0630.

The lower portion of the Detroit River is fairly broad with numerous islands and channels so accurate piloting is critical. Just after we entered the river visibility was limited not only by a dense haze, but also a growing presence of small insects. Eventually, the insects became so thick that they were flying in our noses, ears, mouths, hair, clothes, and were covering the deck. Mr. Singer was at the helm while Chris and I were serving as lookouts. Being the captain, I took advantage of the r.h.i.p. rule* and said to Mr. Singer, "I have to go below and check our position." I shamelessly went down the companionway, leaving Mr. Singer at the helm and Chris on the foredeck to do battle with the little buggers. Oh the relief.

As I was supposedly plotting a position, Mr. Singer yelled, "Hey Corn. What are you doing down there? I gotta get out of this." Fortunately for Mr. Singer, the guilt of taking advantage of my position as captain got the best of me and, I traded positions with Mr. Singer who then, after a short period, in turn traded positions with Chris.

Again, I crawled into this hellhole, of tiny monsters, grabbed the helm and watched enviously as Mr. Singer and Chris now interchangeably sought relief. I don't remember how long this routine went on. Perhaps a half hour, but it seemed like hours. Slowly the little monsters began to dissipate until gone, other than a covering of dead insects and slimy green blotches on the deck, coaming, helm, winches, and sails.

I suppose one of the reasons, other than as mentioned previously, I love to sail with Mr. Singer, he seems to have a way with the gods. No sooner than the insect fiasco occurred, Mr. Singer said, "What we really need now is a torrential downpour." Guess what? Within ten minutes the

---

* Rank has its privileges

sky opened and we had our cleansing downpour. During this downpour, Mr. Singer and Chris both grabbed brushes and scrubbed the deck. Not only that, but within the hour, the sky cleared, the wind picked up from the south at 12 to 15 knots.

The sails were adjusted to wing & wing and we moved at a comparatively high speed (7 knots) northward on the Detroit River. We traveled past open land on both the east (Ontario) and west (Michigan) banks following the buoys that clearly marked the up-bound Amherstburg Channel that runs close to the Ontario mainland and is separated from the down-bound lane called the Livingstone Channel. These two channels are dredged to about twenty-seven feet and are separated by elongated, except for Bois Blanc Island, islands partially formed from the dredging.

The channels merge to the north, where first separated, into a single up-bound and down-bound lane and run north past several islands and subsidiary river channels to the less confused and more easily navigated portion of the Detroit River. At this point the river swings to the north-east past a heavily industrialized area of steel, refinery and manufacturing outlets found in proximity to where the River Rouge empties into the Detroit River.

As we followed the river to the northeast, fortunately the wind turned out of the southwest and we were able to continue wing & wing under the Ambassador Bridge[*] and eventually, past Detroit on the northwest river bank and Windsor on the southeast bank. (The only part of Canada, which lies south of the United States.)

I'm always amazed at how much better a city, town or community looks when viewed from the water including my own metropolitan area of Cleveland. Detroit was no

---

[*] The Ambassador Bridge is one of two auto/truck bridges crossing between the United States and Canada between Lakes Huron and Erie. The second is the Blue Water Bridge at the northern end of the St. Clair River.

different. Perhaps, in the case of a city, the tall majesty of the buildings stands out so starkly. No one can say that Detroit's Renaissance Center is not a truly majestic sight especially with the advantage of being viewed from the water.

"Mr. Singer, do you believe how good the wind gods have been to us? Perfect wind and clear skies." Chris responded, "So far, so good, but we ain't there yet." Mr. Singer then piped up, "Yeah, ya don't wanna anger the wind gods." and then went into a long dissertation about wind and weather. As we approached Belle Isle, located at the northern end of the Detroit River, the wind was shifting westerly causing us to change sails from wing & wing to a beam reach and eventually a close reach*as we proceeded on to Lake Sinclair.

Lake St. Clair is a comparatively small lake and, like the Detroit and St Clair Rivers, permits transit of vessels from the upper lakes to the lower lakes. In addition to the St. Clair River that empties the upper Great Lakes into Lake St. Clair, a number of small rivers and creeks empty into Lake St. Clair. The St. Clair River and the smaller rivers and creeks carry and release an abundance of sediment. Lake St. Clair is extremely shallow and consequently, requires a channel for deep draft vessels to be maintained from where the St. Clair River empties into Lake St. Clair to where Lake St. Clair empties into the Detroit River.

This straight channel is well marked with lighted flashing green buoys and elevated flashing red lights. Transit by deep draft vessels cannot stray, less they would go aground. During the final daylight hours, we continued under sail northeast in the shipping channel until reaching the St Clair River at sundown. As we were about to enter the river

---

*A beam reach is when the wind comes toward a vessel at an angle of 75 to 115 degrees from the bow (across mid-ship). As the wind shifts to less than a 75 degree angle, the vessel is said to be on a close reach. Wind coming from 45 degree angle or less the forward movement of the vessel decreases as the angle decreases.

through the St. Clair Cutoff* the wind continued its shift to the north and we were forced to drop sail and proceed under power.

The St. Clair River is very different from the Detroit River. The lower portion of the Detroit River is broader with numerous islands, inlets, and channels requiring constant attention to landmarks and buoys particularly in the lower portion. The St. Clair River is akin to a straight ditch requiring less attention to the skills of piloting. In making our way northward on the St. Clair River in the darkness of late evening and early morning we motored northward past small Canadian river towns on the east bank and small American river towns on the west bank, passing occasional pleasure boats, work boats, ferries and ore freighters. Finally, at 0330 we arrived and docked at Port Huron, Michigan, the northern most port on the U.S. side of the St. Clair River. We had been under way forty-seven hours and covered 194 nautical miles.** according to the log.*** We didn't want to take much time ashore as we were anxious to leave the confines of the St. Clair River and journey into the comparative vastness of Lake Huron. Exhausted, we all fell into a deep albeit short well deserved sleep prior to a short exploration of Port Huron and sending Chris, by bus, on his way back to Pontiac. Now the major objective in Port Huron was to secure charts of Lake Superior.

---

* At the southern end of the St. Clair River, the river splits into several channels as current slows at Lake St. Clair and sediment is deposited forming low marshy islands. A cut to the main river channel has been made from Lake St. Clair.

** A nautical mile (6076 feet) is equal to 1.15 statute mile (5280 feet).
~ 194 nautical miles times 1.15 equals 223 statute miles.

*** The log on the *Mistress,* as opposed to the written vessel's log is a speed indicator set to measure distance activated by a small paddle wheel located below the water line. The paddle wheel turns from water passing the hull. Since a portion of the trip was against the currents of the Detroit and St. Clair Rivers, the actual distance was somewhat less than that recorded.

After a few hours of wandering through the town in and out of boating equipment stores and questioning locals as to where Lake Superior Charts could be secured, the conclusion was made, the elusive charts were not available in Port Huron.

"Don't worry Mr. Singer. Surely as we travel further north, we'll find charts for Lake Superior."

ContinuingNorth:

Boaters are always exchanging stories of their boating experiences. You listen and learn not only about their experiences, repeat of second and third hand experiences, but also, learn to take so called "experiences" with a grain of salt. As mentioned previously six years before this trip, when I had traveled to Toronto in my former boat *Escape III,* I was exposed to a multitude of stories of the horror of and subsequent advice for transiting the Welland Canal by "experienced" boaters.

Again, "experienced" boaters had their stories, but this time they cautioned going from the St. Clair River under the Blue Water Bridge* onto Lake Huron. This is where water from the upper Great Lakes is funneled into the St. Clair River. "The current is too strong to get out onto Lake Huron." "You'll have to have a power boat tow you out onto Lake Huron. "

After our brief sojourn into the business section of Port Huron, we departed in the afternoon, out into the St. Clair River heading for Lake Huron. As we made our way into the center of the river Mr. Singer said, "Damn, this current is strong." "Yeah," I responded and proceeded to increase

---

* The Blue Water Bridge crosses from the United States to Canada at the northern end of the St. Clair River. It is at this point under the bridge where the fastest current on the navigational waters of the Great Lakes is found.

the engine r.p.m. to no avail as we barely made forward progress. Maybe they were right. Continuing at a higher than usual r.p.m. I steered toward the Canadian shore where the current was not as strong. We began to move forward until finally, after hugging the Canadian shore, we exited the river into the current-less Lake Huron.*

Once in Lake Huron, we proceeded to make our way north approximately 5 to 15 miles off the Michigan shore through the late afternoon, evening and early hours of the morning. Our progress was extremely slow since the wind was light out of the south. At 0445 I took a bearing off the Harbor Beach radio beacon to see if this bearing confirmed our D.R. position.**It did, and thus, we knew our approximate position. We knew that we wanted to head north toward the St. Marys River in order to get to Michipicoten Island. Exactly which northerly direction was dependent upon the wind and our particular fickleness at

the time. "Let's go to Tobermory," suggested Mr. Singer. "Well I don't know," I responded, "Let me check the chart." I went below to the chart table, looked over the Lake Huron chart, made of few calculations and came up and announced to Mr. Singer,

radio direction finder
(r.d.f.)

"That's over 100 miles diagonally across Huron with no navigational aids." "What do you think?" responded Mr.

---

*Some boaters will argue that a current affects navigation on the Great Lakes. While there is a flow of water toward the St. Lawrence River and the ocean, current within the expanses of each of the lakes is imperceptible,

** D.R. stands for dead reckoning. This is a position determined by piloting i.e. combining compass direction, speed, and time giving an estimated position on a chart. A line drawn from the direction of a radio beacon when plotted should pass through or near the estimated position.

Singer. "What's the worst that could happen? If we miss Tobermory, we'll just have to find and tune in a radio beacon or take bearings from land based objects to determine our position. After all, it's not like we were crossing 3000 miles of ocean." The wind was out of the southeast at about 11 knots so we were again able to sail wing & wing.

Tobermory is a small Canadian town located at the northern end of the Bruce Peninsula. The Bruce Peninsula separates Lake Huron from the Georgian Bay. Tobermory is a major stopping port for pleasure craft passing between these two bodies of water. It was decided that our destination would be for the flashing green buoy located approximately one and one half mile northwest of the Bruce Peninsula. This buoy marks the entrance to the Devil Island Channel, which leads from Lake Huron to the Georgian Bay.

We sailed all that evening, the next morning and throughout the day and into the next evening on a heading of 020 degrees. The wind was a light 11 knots with a clear sky and flat sea.

It was at this time Mr. Singer came up with the idea of riding the *Damn Thing* . "Hey! Why don't I get into the *Damn Thing* and take a little ride?" Conditions were optimal for such an endeavor. Mr. Singer grabbed the painter, pulled the *Damn Thing* up to the transom and asked me to hold on to the painter as he climbed over the lifelines and lowered himself into the *Damn Thing* "Let out the painter." I did and for a while had the *Mistress* all to myself as Mr. Singer followed along under-tow about 70 feet to the rear shouting what a great experience *Damn Thing* riding was.

"O.K., reel me in." I brought Mr. Singer up to the transom and watched him climb aboard. "Your turn Corn. That was great." "No, I don't think so." "Go ahead," exclaimed Mr. Singer, "You'll love it." Now generally, Mr. Singer is seldom insistent, but in this instance, he departed from character and holding the *Damn Thing* up to the transom and insisted, "Go ahead and try it."

Reluctantly, I climbed into the *Damn Thing*, Mr. Singer let out the painter, and soon I was enjoying the solitude of being alone in the middle of Lake Huron. Mr. Singer was right. Skimming along in the small *Damn Thing* at four or five knots in the middle of Lake Huron seventy feet from the security of the Mistress was indeed an interesting experience.

Soon after I was safely aboard the *Mistress* and the *Damn Thing* was returned to her normal position, we continued our northerly trek. During the night the wind steadily increased, the sky clouded over, and waves grew to five feet as we sailed through the night and into the next day. At 1745 we spotted land (hopefully the Bruce peninsula) and continued on a heading of 020 degrees.[*]

At 2130 we spotted the flashing green buoy that marked the southwest entrance to the Devil Island Channel. All day and into the evening the wind continued to increase and by now the wind had increased to approximately 30+ knots and waves had built from eight to ten feet. We were tired and anxious to secure shelter as we passed the flashing green buoy and headed up the Devil Island Channel. We were pleasantly pleased that we had been able to sail over 100 miles utilizing only a corrected compass heading. It was comforting to know that the compass heading had been accurate.

---

[*] A compass does not point to true north. There is what is known as magnetic variation that is shown on most charts. In addition, the compass on every vessel is further affected by deviation that is caused by the unique characteristics of the vessel such as the position of the engine and other ferrous (iron) metals relative to the compass. The amount of deviation changes depending on the heading of the vessel and every captain, to pilot successfully, needs to have an accurate deviation table specifically for that vessel. To get true north the compass heading must be added to or subtracted from.

Tobermory:

At 2230, in pitch-blackness, we entered the Devil Island Channel and were beginning to look for range lights* that marked the channel. Since we were going into unknown waters at night, the sails were dropped and we continued under power looking for the range lights marking the channel. "See any lights?" I yelled to Mr. Singer. "Can't see a thing," came the response. Slowly we proceeded through the blackness for there were no lights and the sky was overcast. Slower and slower; throttle down to idling speed. "Where the hell are the range lights Mr. Singer? Are we in the channel?"

I quickly went below to check the chart and make sure we were on a course that would take us up the channel. The course was correct, but still no range lights. Fortunately, by now the wind had died down and the water had become calm. Still no range lights. Are we in the channel? I thought. "Keep her exactly on course," I instructed Mr. Singer. "I'm going forward to look out." There are numerous hazards such as boulders and small islands in the area and we were fearful of running aground or crashing into a submerged boulder. As I Looked into the blackness, I could see nothing. Perhaps we should turn around, return to open water and wait for daybreak before trying to enter Tobermory.

By this time we were barely making way. All of a sudden I saw a distant group of bright white lights over the port bow. It couldn't be a town because to the northwest was the Georgian Bay. I turned aft and shouted, "What do you suppose that is?" Again, looking forward, the lights were gone.

---

* Range lights are made up of two separated lights. The most distant light is higher than the closest light. When the closest (lower) light is viewed directly under the furthest (upper) light the course is determined.

We kept looking in the direction the lights were first observed. Nothing. Still we were moving down the Devil Island Channel trying to see in the blackness. Then in the distance a single white light, then a second white light behind the first, and then several more lights followed.

We finally figured that what we were seeing was a ferry, the *Chi-Cheemaun* (Objibwe for Big Canoe), sailing from Manitoulin Island to Tobermory. The lights being observed and disappearing were those of the *Chi-Cheemaun's* lights passing behind small islands that dot the area. Eventually the *Chi-Cheemaun* passed several miles in front of us heading for what now could be observed as the faint glow of light from Tobermory in the distance. We continued slowly on our original course until we could see the *Chi-Cheemaun's* stern light. The Mistress was then slowly turned to starboard and safely followed the *Ch-Ccheemaun's* course into Tobermory.

As we motored into Little Tub Harbour at midnight we began to look around for a place to tie off the *Mistress.* Off to the port side I saw another sailboat tied off. Coincidentally, it was another Tartan 37. Slowly we came along side, stopped and Mr. Singer began to tie off. Suddenly the hatch of the disturbed vessel opened and a gentleman came on deck. "You guys just relocating from across the harbor," he asked. "No," I responded. "We just came from Lake Huron." "What?" he asked incredulously, "You mean you just came down the Devil Island Channel?" He just shook his head and without waiting for an answer, ducked below. Judging from his reaction he probably thought we were insane. Perhaps he was right.

We went below, enjoyed a couple of beersicles to take the edge off and/or add to our extreme exhaustion, cooked another meal of canned food and collapsed into wonderfully secure sleep.

We had been under way for forty-five hours and traveled a distance of 142 nautical miles according to the log. The final three hours and about 8 miles of this can simply be described as being in a state of excitement, stupidity, wonderment, anxiety and sheer terror.

Early the next morning, a bright, beautiful day, we did, in fact, move north across the harbor to where there was more activity. By this time, Mr. Singer's dry ice was gone and it was time to pack the icebox with ice. Unfortunately, for some reason the truck bringing ice to Tobermory did not show up. No big deal. Most of our food was in cans (soup, beef stew, vegetables) or preserved packages such as Pop Tarts or potato chips. The real tragedy was that our (formerly beersicles) beer would get warm. Fortunately, we found that keeping the beer in a compartment under the forward berth solved this problem. Here the movement of cold evaporating water breaking to either side of the hull would at least keep the beer relatively cool.

Tobermory was, and I suppose still is, a small community isolated at the northern end of the Bruce Peninsula that separates the Georgian Bay from Lake Huron. I can't imagine who lives in or what goes on in Tobermory during the winter season because of its isolation. However, in the summertime the community serves visiting yachtsmen and divers. I was to learn that because of the difficulty of navigating these waters, a number of sunken vessels were found in the area. This coupled with extremely clear unpolluted water drew numerous sport divers. Had I known this, I probably would not have tried to come into Tobermory in the dark especially when I could not see the range lights.

As we were strolling around Tobermory, we met up with a fellow I'll refer to as "Pierre". Pierre was an average looking fellow about 5'10" with dark curly hair and dressed like a north woods lumberman. Pierre had admiringly noticed *Mistress* tied along the quay and inquired in a thick French Canadian accent, "Where are you heading?" "Lake Superior," I responded. "Where are you from?" I queried.

"We, my wife and I, are from Quebec. We drove here trailing our boat so we could sail around North Channel. May I look at your vessel?"

Generally every boat owner is proud to show off his/her vessel. "Sure. Come along." As we walked toward the *Mistress,* Pierre told us how he hoped to someday own a vessel like the *Mistress,* but for now he had to make do with his 22 foot trailerable craft. "Besides," he said, "with limited time off of work, I can travel quickly in many different directions and sail in many different kinds of water." Ah yes, in his own way Pierre had also found a means to escape the hum-drum of work and responsibility.

"Come aboard Pierre" was quickly followed by the snapping open of beer cans mildly warmed due to the lack of ice. Pierre made the traditional inspection followed by the traditional comments such as "Very nice, beautiful workmanship," etc. We engaged in small talk for a short period, while Pierre envied the *Mistress* and our voyage. I admired Pierre's ability to sail such a small trailerable vessel in the North Channel.

Mr. Singer, never at a loss for words, also enjoyed the conversation, but I could tell by his sudden and unusual silence that he was getting antsy. Finally, I thanked Pierre for coming aboard, and told him that we were anxious to get underway the next day and still had to look for charts in Tobermory. "Yes, yes, of course. Perhaps we'll meet again someday." Feeling sorry to have chased him off, I responded, "I certainly hope so. Aue revoir, mon ami."

We then hurriedly began to get organized for departure. We were about to go ashore to look for Lake Superior charts when there came a knocking on the hull. I came up through the companionway to see Pierre standing along the quay. "I brought you something I'm sure you will need when you get to Superior." "What's that?" I asked. With that, Pierre tossed me a couple of small boxes of insect repellant items. These were in the form of a green spiral disk that, when mounted on an accompanying metal holder and lit, would slowly burn around, supposedly keeping away nasty little flying creatures. "Many have told me that insects are bothersome on Lac Superior. Bon voyage." With that, Pierre departed.

Mr. Singer and I rested a little and strolled around Tobermory. The only thing we needed, besides ice, were charts of Lake Superior. I was sure there would be charts of Lake Superior in Tobermory. After all, we were now less than 150 miles from Lake Superior. In addition, at the north side of the harbor was an outlet called the "Mariner Chart Shop". Unbelievably, the "Mariner Chart Shop" did not have any Lake Superior charts.

"Don't worry Mr. Singer. Surely as we travel further north, we'll find charts for Lake Superior."

On to Sault Ste. Marie:

On a Wednesday, 9 July after a good nights sleep, we departed Tobermory at 0915, destination, Sault Ste. Marie. It was overcast as we motored northward out of Tobermory Harbour and into the Georgian Bay northwest past Cove Island, west into the Main Channel. We passed a bell buoy and returned to Lake Huron at about 1115. Winds were light at about six knots out of the west-southwest as we raised sail and headed for the Ducks* about forty miles to the north-west on a course of 295 degrees.

As the day progressed the wind gradually increased and steadied to sixteen knots while the sky cleared. At about 0600 the wind died and we bent the stay-sail** before passing the Ducks about four hours later. By the time we

---

* The Ducks are a small group of islands located south-west of Manitoulin Island (the largest fresh water island in the world).
** The stay sail or tall boy is a light air jib sail that mounts on the deck between the Genoa jib and the mast.

reached the Ducks the wind again increased to sixteen knots out of the southwest. After passing the Ducks we altered course to 303 degrees, which would take us directly to Detour Passage.[*]

Just after midnight the wind again died down and we went under power for several hours. Finally at 0400 we spotted the Detour Light and entered Detour Passage at 0730. As we traveled northward into Mud Bay and north-northwesterly into Munuscong Lake, there is a secondary channel to the east that follows the Canadian shore northward to Lake George also bordering Canada to the east.

It appeared that in past times this route through Lake George may alternately have been utilized by shipping coming down from Lake Superior. Possibly as ships grew larger, deeper drafts, and the demand for iron ore from the Mesabi Range increased, this easterly route would not suffice for shipping. In any event, the deeper more westerly route, as dredged and cuts were made in the channel, is now utilized by commercial shipping. As mentioned, a major portion of this easterly route passes through Lake George, an elongated lake running north-south about ten miles. This route then turns west onto a northern branch of the St. Marys River, extends southwest to intersect with the main commercial course of the St. Marys River and the towns of Sault Ste. Marie, Ontario and Michigan.

As we motored northward and on to Lake George the wind suddenly increased to fifteen knots. Time to recheck the chart and get ready to raise sail. I went below, grabbed the appropriate chart and brought it up on deck. Stupidly, I placed it upon the seat to have a look around this new environment. Whoosh. The beautiful fifteen-knot wind that we had been hoping for blew the chart into Lake George. We really needed that chart now floating on Lake George.

---

[*] Detour Passage is the main shipping channel located between the eastern tip of Michigan's upper peninsula and Drummond Island.

"Oh no, Mr. Singer. We gotta get that chart." I pulled back on the throttle and circled *Mistress* while Mr. Singer pulled the *Damn Thing* up to the stern. He climbed in and I released the *Damn Thing*'s painter. Mr. Singer then made his way to the floating chart and thankfully retrieved it from the water.

After coming back aboard and securing the *Damn Thing,* Mr. Singer's only comment was, "Boy that was a frightening thing to have happen." I responded, "It sure was. From now on, no light-weight paper charts are to leave chart table." And henceforth, they never did.

But now it was time to raise sail and make our way with a fifteen-knot wind to the north end of this protected flat water Lake George. After reaching the north end of Lake George sail was dropped. We then entered the northern artery of the St. Marys River and motored to the town of Sault Ste. Marie, Ontario.

At 2030 we tied up at a Canadian government wharf to be greeted by the Canadian Harbor Master, Mr. Hank Coyle. "Where you boys from?" asked Hank. "Cleveland," responded Mr. Singer who added, "Do you know where we can buy charts of Lake Superior?" "Yes, there's a government office in town." "How far is that?" I asked. "About two miles," responded Hank.

I figured we'd wait until morning and walk into town until Hank asked, "You boys want a ride into town? I think they'll still be open." "Sure do, that would be great," I replied. "Come on then." Hank started to walk past a small house on a hill overlooking the St. Mary River. Sitting out on a front porch was a woman whom I assumed to be Hank's wife. As we passed Hank yelled out officiously, "Gotta take these boys up town to get some charts." She nodded approvingly and we climbed into Hanks old car.

We were able to get the necessary coastal charts of the east end of Lake Superior including Michipicoten Island

and Whitefish Bay, which leads into the St. Mary River. As we got back into Hank's car, I asked, "Where's your favorite watering hole?" Hank responded, "Oh, that's o.k." "Hey," I said, "It's the least we can do. Anyway, we'd also like to get a drink somewhere." Hank had no trouble finding water holes and a good time was had by all.

We finally poured into the sack for a good nights sleep. We had been under way for thirty-five and one half hours and traveled a distance. of 153 nautical miles according to the log. Most importantly, I didn't have to say, "Don't worry Mr. Singer. Surely as we travel further north, we'll find charts for Lake Superior."

On to Michipicoten Island:

The next morning, after finishing breakfast, we looked for Hank Coyle and his wife, but they were not to be seen. We stowed our precious new charts, checked the area chart and got under way at 1100 for the Canadian Soo lock a few yards up stream. Unlike the Welland Canal, which bypasses the Niagara River and Falls and is comprised of a total of eight locks along a forty mile stretch with a drop of 193 feet, the Canadian side of the St. Marys River consists of one lock to bypass the St. Marys rapids, with a rise of 21 feet,[*] little more than an inconvenience.

---

[*] Presently there are also a larger locks on the American side called the Soo Locks that are utilized for the bulk carriers. Originally shipping could not transit from the lower Great Lakes to Lake Superior because of rapids of the St. Marys River. A lock was first constructed in 1798 by the British. However, this lock was destroyed by the U.S. during the War of 1812. In 1855, a second lock was constructed on the U.S. side of the river. This was followed by another lock on the Canadian side of the river in 1895. Presently the super lakers utilize the 1200 feet locks on the American side, while the smaller lock on the Canadian side is used mainly for pleasure craft. The American locks were rebuilt in 1968.

After a few minutes, raising to the Lake Superior level, we proceeded up the St. Marys River and on to Whitefish Bay.[*] As we entered Whitefish Bay we again went under sail as the wind was building to 20 to 30 knots out of the north. In approximately 20 miles we would enter the open water of Lake Superior, the largest, deepest and greatest of the Great Lakes and set a course for Michipicoten Island.

By late in the afternoon the wind was still blowing 20 to 30 knots out of the north as we were now well into Lake Superior with its long swells. We continued throughout the evening past mid-night after which, the wind died down until we were forced to motor. Sailors prefer not to motor, but when the wind drops to zero and we were limited in time rather than sitting in what is comparable to the "horse latitudes"[**] we elected to again go under power.

Throughout the early hours of the morning as Mr. Singer and I traded off turns at the helm, we both traveled below to add layers of clothing. "Got any gloves?" questioned Mr. Singer, who by this time looked like the Michelin tire man as did I due to the numerous layers of clothing. "This wheel is sure getting cold."

Fortunately, I did have gloves, which Mr. Singer went below to retrieve. I called, "While you're down there, check and see what the temperature is," He yelled back, "Would you believe 45 degrees on July 12?" This was at about 0500.

---

[*] Located at the southeastern end of Lake Superior, the Edmund Fitzgerald was hoping to reach its comparatively protected waters before its tragic sinking in November 1976.

[**] On the ocean there is a belt of generally windless areas in both the northern and southern hemispheres. These, in modern times, are referred to as the doldrums. Before engine powered vessels these were often referred to as the "horse latitudes" because so many horses died of heat exhaustion and starvation when being transported to the new world. Often a sailing crew, rowing in a long boat would have to tow the mother vessel out of the doldrums.

On we continued passing Caribou Island to port. It was now overcast and a light drizzle began to occur. By now the swells had subsided, the surface was flat and the wind picked up to 10 knots out of the east.

A faint view of Michipicoten Island was finally spotted about twenty miles in the distance at 1100. I wondered what we would find there. Shortly the rain ceased and the sun came out as we continued slowly northwest. At 1700 we entered Quebec Harbour under sail. While our 1974, Canadian Hydrographic Service (surveyed in 1916), showed buoys marking the channel into the harbor, the channel was actually marked by crude stakes stuck into the bottom.

While I knew the compass course to be sailed into the harbor, I noticed my compass reading was about 15 degrees off of what it was supposed to be. Never the less, I

Stakes mark the channel into Quebec Harbour

followed the channel marked by the stakes thankful that it was still daylight. The chart showed a magnetic variation of over 7 degrees east at the tip of land on the east side of the harbor entrance and almost 14 degrees west at the tip of land on the west side of the harbor entrance.[*]

As we entered the large harbor, I turned east to the head of the harbor where we dropped sail and set anchor. What? No other boats? We were the sole occupants of this magnificent harbor. At least we thought so.

---

[*] Such wide variations within such a small distance are caused by concentrations of iron within the rocky projections.

Shortly after dropping anchor and beginning to secure and tidy up *Mistress,* a small outboard boat came from the north shore and began to circle us. Despite seeing the name and home port on the transom, the small boat occupant asked, "You from Cleveland?" "Yes," I responded. "What was your last port?" I responded, "Sault St. Marie, Canada."

Mr. Singer preparing to drop sail in Quebec Harbour

Mr. Singer then asked, "Where's a general store?" "General store? Hell, there ain't but two human beings on this island, me, the light keeper, and my wife." Mr. Singer's mouth dropped almost, it seemed, to the deck for Mr. Singer and I were running out of cigarettes. I certainly did not relish the thought of spending the next few days with Mr. Singer and me out of cigarettes.

That was our introduction to Gordon Dawson of Michipicoten Island. Gordon Dawson was a rugged looking man with a tanned weather beaten face and sparkly eyes framed by crow's feet. His looks didn't give a clue as to his age. (perhaps, between the age of 40 and 65) He was a stout, muscular man and wore a short-sleeved denim shirt and a cocked nautical type captain's cap. He was a man, as we were to find out, of temperate curiosity and few words.

The light keeper of Michipicoten Island

We had been under way for slightly over thirty hours and traveled a distance of 114 nautical miles since leaving Sault St. Marie according to the log.

Michioicoten Island:

Now secure at our anchorage, it was time to enjoy our beer, cook a well-deserved meal of canned meat stew, vegetables, and crackers while surveying our surroundings.

Quebec Harbour will hold a several anchored boats. The entire harbor was surrounded by woodland and brush. On the south side of the harbor were a few old, weather beaten, graying, wooden shacks, an abandoned log cabin and a dock, remnants of what appeared to be an old fish camp.

It felt good to sit around, relax, and revel in safely reaching our intended goal and drink beer as darkness slowly set in. We discussed plans to go ashore the next day and do some exploration. All of a sudden, as if someone had turned on a switch, insects, mosquitoes, flies or whatever, commenced their evening meal with Mr. Singer and me as the main course. These insects were so voracious that Mr. Singer and I immediately dove below, closed the hatches, covered our selves with blankets and thankfully, as a result of full stomachs including a significant beer buzz, were quickly and mercifully able to fall asleep.

The next day was clear and beautiful. Probably my imagination, but it seemed that being above a latitude of 47 degrees in an unpolluted atmosphere the sunrays were extremely intense and the sky remarkably blue. This is not to say that the July temperature was hot. Lake Superior is large, deep, and cool. We wanted a shower or bath that would not be impossible, but yet uncomfortable by dumping buckets of extremely cold water while on the foredeck.

While cooking breakfast, the silence was broken by Gordon Dawson's skiff coming out to check on us or maybe just engage in conversation. We never met or even saw Mrs. Dawson. Regardless of his quiet disposition it was apparent that Mr. Dawson, while somewhat suspicious of those aboard the *Mistress,* was not adverse to some fresh, albeit one sided, conversation.

"You fellas want to clean up?" he asked. Mr. Singer responded, thinking that maybe Mr. Dawson was inviting us to his house, "Sure do." "Well, if you take your dinghy over to where you entered the harbor, there are large shallow pools in the rocky small islands. By noon these get nice and warm. Perfect for a bath. See ya later." And off he went.

Mr. Dawson's advice was well received. After breakfast and straightening up the *Mistress,* we climbed into the *Damn Thing* with soap and towels and rowed to the entrance channel where small solid rock islands held small shallow pools of water heated by the sun. Two sailors never more enjoyed a warmer most pleasant bath.

Now we were prepared to row over to and tie up at the seemingly forgotten fish camp dock. Climbing out of the

Damn Thing was like stepping back in time. The only indications of modernity were some electrical wires and a television antenna on one of the cabins. Posted on one of the buildings was an old weather beaten

sign that prominently read "CAPTAIN JIM QUEBEC HARBOUR" under which read less prominently "PRIVATE PROPERTY NO TRESPASSING MICHIPICOTEN FISHERIES" still further under that read "OUR HARBOUR MASTER IS RODNEY VARCOE".As we wondered around the fish camp, it appeared that there had not been any activity for several years. The yard of the camp was mowed as if being groomed in case of the return of "Captain Jim", Rodney Varcoe, or employees of Michipicoten Fisheries.

It looked as though the Michipicoten fish camp had been utilized in stages over a period of several years. Several yards from the harbour sat an old abandoned log cabin and out-house (privy). Window frames existed with no

windows, a half opened door and the remnants of a fireplace chimney were indicative of long term neglect. From the presence of a nearby large rusting bollard, it appeared that at one time larger vessels may have been tied off at Quebec Harbour.

Along the harbor edge, less aged clap-board buildings were found. These were boarded up and appeared to have been abandoned for several years.

Nearby and closer to the water in front of a docking area was, what appeared to be a processing barn with a large sliding door. Other doors and windows were also boarded up. Adjacent to this building was an old 1920s style fuel pump for fuel probably stored in tanks within the barn. Underground tanks would not have been possible due to a high water table. Generally, these buildings, unlike the log cabin, appeared structurally sound. We would have liked to know more about this group of derelict buildings, but Gordon Dawson, as mentioned, was not a conversationalist.

The yard around the fish camp was well maintained although scrap wood boards were scattered on un-mowed areas near the water. A large pole lamp was

Fish processing barn at the fish camp

positioned above the dock area while a light wood frame stood in the yard. This frame was probably used to dry fishing nets.

I have often wondered why Gordon Dawson was reluctant to provide any comment or information regarding this old camp. Was he saddened by the fact that the camp had seen better active days? The only thing he told us about the island was that occasionally he would hike through the woods. He said he found a large iron kettle on the north side of the island, but had no idea of its origin or purpose.

When we went back to the fish camp dock, several large black colored fish were noted around the dock pilings. We pulled a fishing rod out of the *Damn*  *Thing* found some worms under some boards of a collapsed cabin and proceeded to drown the worms rather than feed any of the fish. As I laid on the dock looking into the exceptionally clear water I would occasionally bump a worm on the nose of the fish, but to no avail.

Anchored *Mistress* can be seen between buildings

It looked as though we were finished exploring the fish camp and head back to the *Mistress* when a small speedboat came into the harbor and tied up at the old fish camp dock. Three guys got out, surprised to see us and we exchanged the normal conversation, "Where you from? Where are you going?" etc. They were from the mainland about ten miles to the north, out for a joy ride. Fortunately for us they had just run out of beer and we had just run out of cigarettes. Even more fortunate, they had plenty of cigarettes and we had plenty of beer. Barter was quick and to the point and we all were satisfied after which the three climbed into their boat and were off back to the mainland.

I've never been able to figure out Gordon Dawson. What was his role on Michipicoten? I think he was a government employee whose job was to make sure the lights at the eastern and western ends of Michipicoten were in proper order on this potentially dangerous obstacle to navigation. The only thing Gordon Dawson told us about any of the aides to navigation was that the diaphone (fog horn) on the island did not have to be activated manually, but rather came on automatically when the fog set in. He explained, with some wonderment and possibly some fear of being technologically replaced, that the diaphone had a light beam directed between two points. When fog set in, the light beam was cut off which in turn activated the diaphone.

Was Gordon Dawson the caretaker for the Michipicoten Fisheries fish camp? As mentioned, the lawn in the vicinity of the camp was mowed. When the mainland visitors left, Gordon Dawson inspected the camp area to make sure that no rubbish was left behind.

Back to the *Mistress*. We were finished exploring what ever there was to explore on the island. The remainder of the island was made up of woodland except for Gordon Dawson's house on the north side of the harbor. Somehow we felt that this side of the harbor was out of bounds.

Captain "Corn" (rowing) and Mr. Singer return to the *Mistress* in the *Damn Thing*

That evening Mr. Singer prepared another meal of canned something or other. As we sat in the Mistress sipping our beer and watching the sun go down we realized that before it was too late, we wanted to close up the cabin and escape the ravishes of the evening insect population. After closing up, we lit a couple of the insect repellant coils supplied by our newfound acquaintance Pierre in Tobermory and drifted into sleep.

The next morning I prepared a breakfast of coffee, bacon and eggs. When in this kind of surrounding and circumstance, all food seems to taste delicious. Again, Gordon Dawson came out and circled the *Mistress*. "What're you fellas up to today?" he inquired. "Nothing much. Guess we'll take off back to Sault St. Marie sometime today." I responded. "You fellas want some ice?" queried Gordon Dawson. "That would be great." I responded. "O.K. I'll see you ashore (meaning the fish camp) in a little while. Bring a plastic garbage bag." With that Gordon Dawson took off to attend to his responsibilities, what ever they were.

We then began to cleanup and plot a course back to Sault Ste. Marie. Finally, about noon Gordon Dawson showed up at the fish camp dock. Mr. Singer and I hopped into the *Damn Thing* and rowed to the fish camp dock. Gordon Dawson, as usual never a man of many words said, "Follow me," as he walked over to the barn. He slid open a well insulated door and inside was a pile of ice crystals, obviously collected during the previous winter. "Hold open your bag," he ordered and Mr. Singer and I reacted accordingly while Gordon Dawson shoveled ice crystals into our plastic garbage bag.

The supply of ice added even more to the mystery of the fish camp. Was this ice kept to supply fishing boats? Was one of Gordon Dawson's jobs to keep ice available in case a fishing boat showed up? We were never able to get an answer from Gordon Dawson.

"Gee, this is great. Can we pay you something?" I asked. No response. We carried the cold bag down and into the *Damn Thing.* Again, I asked, "Can we pay you for the ice?" Gordon Dawson got into his skiff and said, "Have a good trip." started his outboard and motored to his home situated on the north side of the harbor. I guess the ice was Gordon Dawson's, a man of few words, way of saying "Goodbye".

Return to Sault Ste. Marie:

We finally departed Quebec Harbour at 1530. The sun was bright in a cloudless sky as we motored our way through the stakes that marked the channel out of the harbor. Once out of the harbor we rounded the two small islands that protect the Quebec Harbour entrance from a south wind, raised sail to a ten-knot wind out of the east and set a course for Whitefish Bay.

As darkness fell, we continued to trade off manning the helm under a clear sky and gently rolling swells. While each of us manned the helm, the other plotted positions based on our heading and the nautical mileage registered on the log. Shortly after mid-night Mr. Singer decided to go below and catch a few winks while I again manned the helm for a few hours.

I am extremely reluctant to describe what happened next. Bear in mind that we had eaten a few hours before darkness and beer was not on the menu. While manning the helm in the total darkness at about 0200, I saw a flashing green light dead ahead. I couldn't imagine what a flashing green light was doing miles off shore. Was this a lit buoy that somehow had gotten loose? Still coming closer, I finally yelled to Mr. Singer, "Mr. Singer, better get up here." Now we were almost upon the thing. "Mr. Singer, get up here quick." I decided to leave what ever it was on the port side and as I passed it, it was now about three or four feet below the water still flashing green. Finally, Mr. Singer barely awake stumbled up from below, and unfortunately, without his glasses. As I looked astern the flashing green light was now white, came out of the water into the sky and circled to the west at what appeared to be a high speed and disappeared. All I saw was the light. No sound. Unfortunately, without his glasses and half awake, Mr. Singer saw nothing.

I have pondered this experience for several years. Could it be something naturally phosphorescent? If so, why did it turn white upon leaving the water? Could this have been a new secret military weapon? Perhaps, a submersible aircraft? At first, this seemed to be a potentially possible explanation. What better place to test a secret weapon? Any boat approaching would show up on radar. Any boat that is, except a sailboat that is stealth to radar. Other than an ore boat, who would be in the center of Lake Superior in the middle of the night? I think this possible explanation is negated by the fact that there was no sound.

We all can guess at another possible explanation that I am reluctant to mention. I can only describe what I alone saw. As I think back to this experience, I have often wished three things. I wish I knew what I saw, I wish Mr. Singer had on his glasses, and I wish I had never witnessed whatever it was I saw. I hate the fact that I will never know or be able to explain what it was.

For the next few hours there was silence as we made our way toward Whitefish Bay. There was nothing to say. I had seen something that was inexplicable while Mr. Singer had not seen a thing.

We continued sailing throughout the morning darkness as fog developed about 0400 despite the windy condition. With a comparatively dense fog, and being in a major shipping lane it was time to raise the radar reflector. After raising the radar reflector, I turned on the deck light and looked up between the sails. Fog was streaming between the sails like I had never seen before. I had been in fog before, but never with this much wind. Mr. Singer and I both sat quietly observing this phenomena when Mr. Singer commented, "Wow! This is just like I would imagine sitting on an airplane wing in the clouds."

We continued under sail all through the day as the fog slowly dissipated. Late in the day we spotted the light that marked the end of Whitefish Point and the entrance to Whitefish Bay. Continuing southeast under sail we were anxious to reach the buoyed channel entrance to the St. Marys River. We entered the shipping channel, started the engine and dropped sail. It was getting late and I wanted to get down the river and into the Canadian lock before dark. "Corn, why don't you try to call the lock master on the radio?" Good idea and I made contact with the Canadian lock.

The lock personnel advised that they were about to shut down for the evening but would remain if we would hurry. At this point I did something that I seldom do. When on the water, if available, I like to stay within the shipping lanes (usually depths in excess of twenty feet) despite the fact that the draft of the *Mistress* is only four feet. Besides the shipping channels are well marked and staying within the channel negates the possibility of going aground.

"Mr. Singer, rev up the engine. They said they would remain open if we would hurry." As Mr. Singer increased the r.p.m., I checked the chart to determine if we could save some time. Further to the southeast the shipping channel made an abrupt turn to the east-northeast before entering the confines of the St. Mary's River. We could save a little time by cutting across out of and back into the channel. I plotted a course to make this cut noting that the chart indicated a minimum depth of seven feet. "Mr. Singer, turn east. We're going to cut across to save some time." Mr. Singer, knowing my sailing habits, questioned, "Are you sure?"

One of the advantages we have in sailing together is that each double-checks the other in plotting courses, checking positions, and identifying navigational aids. When I returned to the helm, Mr. Singer went below to double check. "Yeah, looks like we shouldn't have a problem."

We made the passage without incident and returned to the buoyed channel and passed through a narrow cut in the shipping channel framed by Point aux Pins on the Canadian side and Brush Point on the Michigan side. The next three miles passed quickly and we were rewarded with open gates to the Canadian lock at 2050.

Shortly after entry into the lock and the gate was closed we dropped the twenty-one feet into the lower portion of the St. Mary River and exited through the east gate of the lock. By now darkness was approaching combined with an almost instantaneous fog as we motored into the small bay to the east of the lock. Visibility became non-existent. We motored slowly, attempting without success to see a dock, land or anything to establish a position. Soon we were heading southeast away from the lock we could no longer see, wary of the area to the southeast where there would be possible traffic to or from the Soo Locks on the American side.

"What'ya think Mr. Singer?" "I think we should sit tight until we can see something," came the response. With those words we began to hear a series of rapid clank, clank, clank off in the distance to the southeast. "Sounds like the freighters are dropping anchors. They must have shut down the whole system." "I think you're right Mr. Singer. Probably we should do the same and wait for clearing. "

Despite our agreement to "sit tight" we bobbed around occasionally moving *Mistress* just barely making way for an undeterminable period. The silence, except for slow reverberation of the engine, was deafening. So not as to stray from what was felt to be a relatively safe area *Mistress,* when moving, was kept in a pattern of making slow tight circles. This procedure went on and on.

Then very slowly out of the fog, less than five feet away, a buoy came into view. "Take the helm, Mr. Singer. I'm going below to see if I can figure out our position. Circle around and for God's sake, don't lose sight of the buoy." After determining our position, I plotted a course from the buoy to the same dock where we previously had tied up. Coming up from the chart table, I told Mr. Singer the compass course to follow as he slowly turned and very slowly headed for the intended dock. I went forward on the deck waiting and watching for anything to come into view. When we were within a few feet, our objective came into view.

At 0100, once safely secured, again a few beers, a hastily cooked meal of the ever-tasty canned food and a collapse into a deep, uninterrupted sleep. We had traveled over 130 nautical miles to the lock in just over thirty hours. Our trip from the lock to our dockage, a distance of about one mile, took over three hours.

The Sault Ste. Marie Incident:

The next day we treated ourselves by sleeping in and awakened to another beautiful clear blue sky. The fog having burned off, the American Soo Locks were again in operation. Time to stow gear, check lines, rearrange charts and say one last "hello" and "goodbye" to Mr. Hank Coyle. After all was secure, we walked up to Hank Coyle's small house overlooking the river. Unfortunately, neither Mr. nor Mrs. Coyle were about.

While we were anxious to get under way, Mr. Singer noted that our beer supply had dwindled substantially as a result of our bartering session on Michipicoten. Better get into town to re-supply. "Wonder where Hank is?" I questioned. "Looks like his car is gone." replied Mr. Singer. "Well, Mr. Singer, let's walk up to town to the local brewery. It's a long way to Cleveland."

We began our walk up from the harbor to the main road leading into the downtown area. Sault Ste. Marie, Ontario reminded me of an old frontier town, a main street with two story buildings with retail outlets on the ground floor with offices and residences on the second floor. We walked briskly down the main drag passing primarily small store outlets. Without saying anything to each other we both noticed a pool hall across the street with several young men hanging around inside and out. We must have appeared to them as being very "yachty" with our shorts, boating shoes and sunglasses.

A few blocks down the street we entered an establishment and proceeded to purchase two cases of Sault St. Marie's finest. Now back to the *Mistress* to restock and get under way. About a block past the pool hall Mr. Singer said to me, "Don't look now, but I think we're being followed by about four or five guys from the pool hall." "I noticed the same thing. What'll ya think we should do?" I said.

Remember Mr. Singer and I had just successfully sailed about close to nine hundred miles in twelve days. We overcame numerous handicaps including a massive bug attack on the Detroit River, beating the current of the St. Clair River, conquering the Devil's Island Channel, losing a chart on Lake George, fighting occasional storms, surviving an instantaneous fog and effecting, if I do say so myself, excellent navigation. In short, we were feeling rather cocky and no one was about to relieve us of our beer.

Mr. Singer said "I'm going to rest my case of beer on your case." He did and then proceeded to reach inside the case, pulled out a bottle and then grabbed the case back. "Now rest your case on top of mine and pull out a bottle. We may be outnumbered, but we'll take a couple with us." Blindly and stupidly I followed Mr. Singer's instruction. We both were of a single mind. If they wanted our beer, they would have to pay dearly.

Fortunately, especially for us, the pool hall gang, having watched our maneuvers with the bottles, decided that maybe we were not such an easy mark or perhaps did not want to experience the wrath of Hank Coyle as we turned into Mr. Coyle's front yard on our way back to the *Mistress.* They then proceeded to turn and head back to the pool hall. Whatever the reason, we enjoyed the macho feeling that was derived from retaining our precious beer supply without conflict. Oh, the stupidity of middle aged guys.

Return to Lake Huron:

Returning to the *Mistress* we got under way at 1330, down-bound into Lake Nicolet.* The wind was out of the northwest at fifteen-knots and once again we were able to sail wing & wing. We continued south and south-southwest the full length of Lake Nicolet. After examining the chart, Mr. Singer announced that we should think about changing from wing & wing since we were about to abruptly change course. I thought for a minute and said, "Let's wait until we make the change in course to see what happens." As we changed course the wind remained at our back as though being funneled down the St. Marys River valley. Thus, we were able to continue wing n wing.

Within a relatively narrow cut, we noted that two young ladies were observing our progress from atop of a pile of dredge tailing. They waved and Mr. Singer jokingly shouted, "Wanna go south?" With that, both young ladies began to scurry down the rubble intent, I guess, on heading south. "What're you nuts?" I shouted to Mr. Singer. "That's all we have to do is pick up a couple of young ladies, the age of which we don't know. We'd probably get arrested at Detour Village for kidnapping. Besides, I don't want to have to change sail when we're moving so well." At this, Mr. Singer and I both shared a good laugh.

While proceeding south we spotted a down-bound freighter to our rear. We were still under sail and ever so slowly the freighter was gaining on us. "Think we'll beat him to Detour Passage?" questioned Mr. Singer. "I don't know. He probably has a speed limitation on the St. Marys, but slowly he seems to be narrowing the gap." On we sailed as the distance between us shortened. Just before reaching Detour Passage, the freighter eased pass us and much to our

---

* It should be noted that generally the area between Whitefish Bay and Detour Village is referred to as the Saint Marys River. However, some broad expanses along this route are referred to as lakes.

amazement, several of the crew stood at the fan-tail and gave us an unexpected round of applause. We weren't sure why this occurred, but we guessed they had been watching the unofficial race down the river and appreciated our effort to keep ahead while under sail.

About 1730 the sky was overcast as we again passed Detour Village and made our way into Lake Huron after which we turned west heading for the Straits of Mackinac. We had discussed this diversion and thought it would significantly add to our experience and bragging rights if we could claim to have sailed four of the five Great Lakes within two weeks.

I went below and began to cook another one of those delicious meals of canned food. While doing so, it dawned on me that this was already the middle of the second week of the voyage. I brought a bowl of food and coffee to Mr. Singer and said, "You know it's already the middle of the second week of the voyage!" "Yeah, I know. What are you thinking Corn?" "I'm thinking we'd better forget about Lake Michigan and start making our way south. We both have to go back to work in less than a week." Reluctantly, but realistically, Mr. Singer agreed and at 2130 we turned to the southeast.

That evening a dense fog accompanied the darkened sky and up went the radar reflector as numerous freighters were going to or coming from the St. Marys River or the Straits of Mackinac. All night and until late in the morning we could hear the horns of the passing freighters as they made their way through the fog. We were truly thankful for the reflective properties of a radar reflector.

By 1100 a light five-knot wind had shifted to the southeast and we began to tack to make progress to the southeast. The fog was patchy near the surface while deceptively overhead, a bright blue sky prevailed. The Michigan shore appeared to be five or six miles to the west. I was at the helm while Mr. Singer was relaxing and just happened to look over the side. "Hey Corn, I can see the bottom boulders." I quickly looked over the side and confirmed Mr. Singer's observation. "Let's do a 180 and get away from here." We turned to the opposite direction and made our way into deeper water.

After carefully reviewing the chart, it was determined that we were indeed in comparatively shallow water five to six miles off shore. The shallowest depth was twenty-two feet, no threat to the *Mistress,* but with clear water and the sun shining down we saw large boulders which gave us cause for alarm and resulted in our heading due east away from land.

Patchy fog continued for the remainder of the day as the sky became overcast and threatening. We sailed east for several hours back into the easterly limits of the shipping lanes before turning southwest. We wanted to enter Thunder Bay, but had to be sure we were far enough south to pass North Point at the end of a peninsula that forms the northeast portion of Thunder Bay. Once around North Point we could then head northwest approximately nine miles to Alpena, Michigan. Perhaps we would be lucky enough to reach shelter before the heavens opened.

No such luck. While the weather had been threatening all day, as we entered Thunder Bay in the early evening, a torrential rain accompanied by bolts of lightening and claps of loud thunder greeted us.* The surface of the bay was not particularly rough since the bay was well protected and

---

* There are many misconceptions with regard to lightning. When properly grounded, a boat has what is called a cone of protection that offers protection against a lightning strike. I've heard boaters claim that they disconnect their radios during lightning storms to protect the radio from being blown out by lightning. One year I was in Rondeau Harbour, Ontario on the north side of Lake Erie when two boats were struck while at dockside. I came to find out that they had disconnected their radios. I theorized that when they disconnected their marine radios they eliminated the radio ground and thus, made their vessels susceptible to lightning strikes,

heavy rain tends to flatten the surface. Wind was out of the southeast, which was perfect as we continued north, soaked from head to toe. Visibility improved as slowly the fog had dissipated. No other vessels were spotted.

The fact that we had an aluminum mast projecting over fifty-feet above the surface of the water was not of particular concern. We had often experienced storms of this magnitude and had complete faith in the fact that *Mistress* was well grounded. Still, lightening and thunder can be disconcerting especially when out on the open water. Mr. Singer, as mentioned previously, not a man of vocal brevity, looked at me and appropriately commented, "Why do you think they call it Thunder Bay?"

Alpena, Michigan:

About 2030 we entered the small boat harbor at Alpena. We had sailed a distance of 136 nautical miles in thirty-one hours. Not realizing that I was at a commercial dock a person came to meet us and inform us of the docking fee. I told the individual that I was a member of the Chagrin Lagoons Yacht Club east of Cleveland. Rather than telling me I was not at the Alpena Yacht Club that was across the way, in keeping with a true capitalist mentality, the person merely said, "Doesn't matter, you still have to pay for dockage." I was too tired to argue and paid the appropriate fee. Reeling under the impact (not the cost, but rather the principle) of having to pay for dockage at what I thought was a yacht club, I went below and emotionally told Mr. Singer, "Damn it! They made me pay for dockage. Turn on every light on the boat. Let's use up the electricity for which we're paying."

I had been to Alpena on a business trip a few years earlier, but as usual when approached from the water communities seem to take on a different character and nothing appeared recognizable. It was getting late, but fortunately the saloons would be open. Sure enough we found a nearby watering hole and began consumption of the "demon rum" until closing hour. As we made our way back to the *Mistress,* while crossing a bridge, we ran into two locals who had also been imbibing in something stronger than Kool Aid.

Aggressively one of the two asked, "Where (hic) the hell are you guys going?" Right away the hair on Mr. Singer's neck bristled. "What's it to ya?" responded Mr. Singer equally aggressive. The other stood by without uttering a word. Oh, oh. Looks like a fight is brewing, I thought and jumped in with, "Where the hell are you guys going?" "We're looking for a (hic) bottle opener," as he held up one of two six-packs of bottled beer. I responded, "I'll show you how to open those bottles without a bottle opener if you'll share two of those beers with us." Curiosity peeked as one of the two handed me a six-pack. I pulled out a bottle, rested the cap on the edge of the steel bridge rail with one hand, pounded down the cap with the other hand and handed an open bottle back to the amazed, formerly aggressive, individual. (I thought everybody knew how to do that.)

"Wow! (hic) That's really amazing. You guys want a beer?" We now shared a couple of beers with our newly found best friends before saying our good byes and making our way back to the *Mistress* without incident.

The next morning, we were understandably slow to start moving. It was already, Thursday, July 17 as we reviewed charts and determined we still had to cover nearly three hundred nautical miles. "Mr. Singer, we only have a few days left. We'd better get going if we're going to make it back in time to go to---" I hesitated momentarily, almost sick to say the word, "work."

The Long Voyage:

We finally departed Alpena at 1230 under a dark overcast sky. Upon reaching the outer channel buoy marking the entrance to Thunder Bay we set a course of 155 degrees to make our way off shore and pass the wide expanse of Saginaw Bay located to the southwest. As the day progressed the sky began to clear during the early afternoon. Winds were light and variable and we oscillated between sail and motoring when the wind died down.

Mr. Singer proposed what he referred to as the "three knot rule". That is, when the wind propelling the *Mistress* falls to a point where the *Mistress* is making way at less than three knots, the iron kicker (engine) should come on. Sailors love to sail and often stubbornly wait for long periods of time before giving in and (unless racing, of course) cranking on the engine. As mentioned in an earlier chapter previously, on my former boat, when returning from Dunkirk, New York, I ran into one of these calm periods at night and sat off of Erie, Pennsylvania for over eight hours without a breath of air. Fortunately, while becalmed, I was exposed to my one and only viewing of the northern lights. This, however, did not compensate for the hours of sitting becalmed. Hard to believe that on a ten thousand square mile body of water a period of calm can last so long Eventually, I gave up on my purist sailing attitude, and with the help of Mr. Singer adopted the "three knot rule". Besides, we were now in a race against time. The "three knot rule" was completely appropriate.

At 0300, the Pte. aux Barques light came into view which meant that we were past Saginaw Bay. We continued on a course of 155 degrees for a few hours and then changed course to 180 degrees, due south to the entrance of the St. Clair River.

Throughout the morning, until late in the afternoon, the wind was nil and we continued motoring due south. At 1500 the wind picked up to 15 knots from the southeast and we joyfully raised sail and bent the staysail for our last hours on Lake Huron. As we approached the buoys marking the shipping channel to the St. Clair River the wind continued to shift to the south and we entered the river at 1730 with the wind on the nose.

"Why in the hell does the wind always blow in the opposite direction of travel on the St. Clair River?" I commented. "Don't complain," responded Mr. Singer. "We've had beautiful weather and besides we now have the current with us and can barrel down without hugging the shoreline," which is exactly what we did.

We spent the next four hours motoring down the St. Clair River without incident occasionally passing an ore boat and the small international ferries carrying passengers between Canada and the United States.

At 2140, we exited the St. Clair Cutoff and were able to sail southwest across Lake St. Clair in about four hours with a ten to fifteen knot southerly wind.

We entered the Detroit River at about 0130 and began passage downstream under power. Despite the fact that we had been under way for thirty-seven hours and covered a distance of approximately 171 miles, we both felt pretty good and decided to continue past Detroit and once again into the Fighting Island Channel. We continued down the Fighting Island Channel to where the fighting Island Channel divides into the Amherstburg and Livingstone Channels. Then down the westerly Livingstone Channel (previously we had come north by way of the easterly Amherstburg Channel) and into Lake Erie.

As usual we traded off double checking each other's navigation particularly with the multitude of lights, buoys, shallow areas, alternate channels, islands and miscellaneous obstructions found within the lower reaches of the Detroit River all this at night complicated by a confusion of backscatter lighting.

As we were following the channel out into Lake Erie, from the chart table, I yelled a course to Mr. Singer just as a large ore boat was crowding us in the channel. "You're wrong Corn. That course will put us right toward land." I checked the chart again and repeated the course to Mr. Singer. "Can't be. Come up here and take a look," Mr. Singer yelled back. When I came up I saw that Mr. Singer was right. Apparently, the nearby ore boat was laden with iron ore that in turn affected the compass. When the ore boat had passed, no longer was our compass reading incorrectly.

As we made our way into Lake Erie we had traveled nearly 200 miles in a period of approximately 42 hours. No longer were we required to intensely concentrate on navigation and welcomed the open water of Lake Erie. The wind was now out of the south at about fifteen knots and the lake was developing a ten-foot chop. Sails were set and we again headed for the Pelee Passage. With that in mind Mr. Singer announced "Corn, I can't take it anymore. I've got to get some sleep." Mr. Singer disappeared below.

Hell, I'm just as tired, I thought. How in the hell am I going to sail and navigate without falling asleep? By now Mr. Singer was completely out. Then I had a revelation. Directly ahead was the ore boat that had passed us coming out of the Detroit River. He's got to be heading to the Pelee Passage. That's it. I'll stay on the same course and follow as long as I can see him. The sails were trimmed and the helm brake set. I constantly dozed and was awakened each time *Mistress* fell off and the sails began to flutter. Doze off, awaken, doze off. Finally, no longer could I see the ore boat heading for the Pelee Passage. "Keep *Mistress* on the same heading." Soon, during one of my brief partially awakened periods, I could make out another ore boat in the distance heading toward me. She too had to come through the Pelee Passage. What a way to navigate.

Finally, after several hours, Mr. Singer popped up from the cabin. "Wow did I need that. How you doin?" With that, I pointed to a ship in the distance and said, "Head for that. She's coming from the Pelee Passage." After which I also collapsed below for a couple of hours.

I was finally awakened by Mr. Singer who yelled, "Hey Corn, we're approaching Pelee Passage." Amazing what a few hours sleep will do. The weather was clear, wind out of the southwest at ten knots and the lake had about a seven-foot chop. At a little past 1100 we passed the Southeast Shoal Lighthouse marking the end of the Pelee Passage. Now we would be on open water until we reached home.

"Hey Corn, don'cha think we out to scrub down the deck? After all, we want to pull into Chagrin Lagoons with every thing looking ship shape and in Bristol fashion."[*] "Yeah, I suppose so," and with that we got out the soap and cleaning bucket with a long lanyard for dipping into the lake. While the lake surface had flattened, the wind continued steady at ten knots out of the southwest and the wheel brake was applied so one could scrub while the other poured copious amounts of lake water across the deck. After scrubbing down the deck, punctuated with a few beers, the last meal was cooked underway.

About 1330, we spotted the smoke stacks of the electric power company that sits adjacent to Chagrin Lagoons. Continuing on a course of about 107 degrees, we finally entered the mouth of the Chagrin River and tied up at 1930, on 19 July 1980. Since leaving Alpena, Michigan we had traveled 275 nautical miles over a period of fifty-five hours.

We sat at the dock contemplating what we had accomplished 1145 nautical miles (1317 statute miles) in a little over fifteen days with seven overnight dockings. "Well, Mr. Singer, at least we'll have tomorrow to readjust to shore life before returning to---," again, I hesitated momentarily, almost sickened to say the word, "work."

---

[*] Bristol fashion is a term meaning that every thing is well cared for on a vessel.

"Think we ought to call the women?" asked Mr. Singer matter-of-factly. "That sounds like a good idea," came my response. Within one hour, the women (Carol my wife and Renee, later to become Mrs. Singer) came aboard. Renee presented each of us with a pewter tankard engraved "Cornell & Singer Lake Superior & Back 1980" for me and "Singer & Cornell Lake Superior & Back 1980". Renee explained the difference in the engraving was due to our very large egos.

No matter. It was now our turn to sit in the yacht club and tell numerous tales of adventure on the high seas. Tales, as I mentioned earlier, about going through the Welland Canal and fighting upstream under the Blue Water bridge, must be taken with a grain of salt and experienced before being taken as fact. Oddly enough, when hearing about the trip, generally the reaction was not that of admiration or even disbelief, but rather, "You guys must be nuts."

About a week later, we ran into one of the older club members. He took the wind out of our sails quickly when he said, "Heard about your trip up north. I suppose that next year you're planning on something really big." Gee, we thought we had just done something really big.

MISTRESS Sails North
July 1980
William E. Cornell, Jr.

The Bahamian Incident

Most sailors, it seems, are always looking for ways to expand their sailing experiences. I had sailed extensively on the Great Lakes, but I still wanted the additional experience of some salt water sailing. While spending much time in Florida conducting business for the company I worked for (Sherwin-Williams), I asked one of my representatives to see if he could find a boat for us to sail across to the Bahamas.

A few weeks later, I sat in my yacht club soaking up a Cuba-Libre to stem off the cold of a December afternoon. Since there is no boating activity in northern Ohio this time of year, the only thing to do was sit around the bar and tell sea stories, both true and false. In the middle of one of these stories, in walks John. John had retired and had taken his 36 foot Pearson called *Katz 'N Jammer* south along the Inter-coastal Waterway to Fort Lauderdale, Florida.

"How're you doing John? How are things in Florida?" The usual yacht club bar talk continued. "Gee, you're looking a little down John. What's wrong?" John looked up from his drink and said, "Oh, I can't find anyone with guts enough to go across to the Bahamas with me." Wow! Just perfect. I could hardly wait to tell John, "Your search is over. I have one of my guys Greg looking for a boat for us to go across. He's a good guy and would be good crew." John hesitated for a moment and said, "Yeah, and I could get my son Jack to go along with us." "O.K. I'll be back in Florida in the next few weeks and we can all get together and see if we get along."

A few weeks later we were able to get together on John's boat in Fort Lauderdale and every one hit it off well. Greg worked under me as a corporate real estate representative. He was originally from Chicago and I believe graduated from college on a baseball scholarship. Jack, was a motorcycle enthusiast, complete with "black leather jacket with an eagle on the back". Jack worked as a Rolls Royce auto mechanic in Miami.

Jack and Greg, despite unusually different backgrounds, found commonality in the fact that they were both scuba divers. They planned on doing some diving when we got to the Bahamas.

That evening we all wound up at a biker bar familiar to Jack. I think the bar was called something like "Big Tuna". John said they were a pretty rowdy bunch, but were basically good guys. "Don't be surprised if the cops come in and make everyone lean up against the wall." They didn't, but one of the big grungy looking guys, noting my non-conforming attire, walked up and said in a gravely sounding voice, "What're you doing here?" Before I could say anything Jack walked up and said, "Back off, he's with me." And so he did. This is the story of my introduction to night-life in Fort Lauderdale or as it came to be known to me as Fort Liquordale.

Filled with anticipation, I returned to Ohio, and acquired a cruising guide to the Bahamas. I carefully familiarized myself with the general positions of several hundred islands and cays. It would be great to visit some of these and explore the area. I knew the low profiles of the Bahamas (coral reefs) would be quite different from the high profiles of the Virgin Islands (volcanic mountain tops).

About three weeks later we joined up again at the *Katz 'N Jammer*. We met in the afternoon, had a few drinks and headed back to the biker-bar. The next day Captain John got things semi organized and we loaded up provisions, booze and scuba gear. Finally, after a decent night's sleep, we were off the next morning. Jack, in his black leather jacket who looked like he should be astride a motorcycle, was at he helm getting a kick out of waving to boaters. Slowly we motored down the channel and into the Atlantic.

John had a worried look as we began to raise sail. "I don't like these conditions. The wind is out of the north and cuts across the Gulf Stream. It's too rough. We're going to turn back." Good God, I thought, this is a cakewalk compared to what I've been through on Lake Erie. Keep your mouth shut Cornell. You never tell another how to run his boat unless he asks.

We made our way back into the Intracoastal Waterway
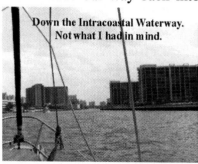
Down the Intracoastal Waterway. Not what I had in mind.

and started heading south. The motoring trip toward Miami, while initially interesting to observe the numerous luxurious buildings, was not what had been anticipated. On we motored until reaching Biscayne Bay and anchoring in a place called No Name Harbor.

That evening we wandered the comparatively deserted shore line and began the earnest consumption of the demon rum. There was nothing else to do except watch helicopters with bright search-lights circle overhead. We weren't sure what they were looking for, but assumed they were some kind of law enforcement looking for drug smugglers. Apparently, slow moving sailboats were above suspicion.

The following day we slept in, attempting to cure the result of too much cheer the night before. Again, throughout the day and into the second evening we wandered the comparatively deserted shore-line. With nothing else to do, again we began the earnest consumption of the demon rum. Gosh, I thought, here I'm giving up a weeks vacation to sit around on an anchored boat, occasionally wander a deserted shore, and drink with captain John and our equally bored crew. Keep your mouth shut Cornell. You never tell another how to run his boat unless he asks.

Just after dark, which by this time we all were a little more than inebriated, Jack pipes up with, "Damn it, you've been talking for months about crossing over to the Bahamas. Here we are with Cornell, an experienced sailor, and two young healthy guys. If we don't leave soon, you'll never go." Jack, I thought, you took the words right out of my mouth. I couldn't say it, but Jack could. The next morning we were up at 0400 and made our way into the Gulf Stream and come to think of it into "the Devils Triangle". Next stop, the Bahamas.

Navigation was simplified by the fact that Captain John had a g.p.s. (geographic position system). In using the g.p.s., Captain John programmed in the latitude and longitude of our destination and followed the course read out. Even though we were crossing the Gulf Stream (about 3 knots setting to the north) the g.p.s. would always read out the course to the destination. A more accurate and shorter crossing could have been accomplished by setting a course correction of a few degrees off the destination to allow for the current of the Gulf Stream (creation of a vector triangle). The closer the destination, the less the course correction.

Katz 'N Jammer at the customs dock of Cat Key, Bahamas

The crossing was uneventful and we finally arrived at an island called Cat Cay. Cat Cay was primarily a private island with a customs installation set up for the benefit of wealthier travelers to the Bahamas. After checking in with a rather officious custom officer we elected to go ashore.

We were soon informed that the island was private and that our exploration was limited to an area along the harbor adjacent to the custom office. We hopped into the dinghy and made our way back to the *Katz 'N Jammer* where we would remain for the next two days. Because we had delayed our crossing for several days, we did not have the time to travel to other islands and had to entertain ourselves aboard the *Katz 'N Jammer*.

We had heard stories about how some vessels were pirated by drug runners, and the occupants murdered. When the vessels had served their illicit purpose the vessels were

then scuttled to avoid detection. Captain John was not about to take any chances and it was decided that at least one of us would alternately stand two hour watches in the cock-pit throughout the night to warn

Jack & Greg-the divers

away any approaching vessel. To back us in this endeavor, Captain John kept a Mini 14 semi-automatic and a shot-gun aboard. Pirating did occur, but I'm now sure that it only occurred in distant isolated islands of the Bahamas.

The next day Jack and Greg decided to get out the scuba gear and do some diving while I decided to go swimming. During their dives they brought up some conch shells and deposited them into the cockpit before concluding their brief dive in about twelve feet of water.

We all climbed aboard and decided we could empty the conchs by inserting an ice pick and spiral out the meat. Unfortunately, one of the larger conchs slipped out of my hand and overboard. Jack and Gregg looked at me and then at each other. With that, Greg handed me a face-mask and it was understood with out a word spoken that I would retrieve this largest of the conch shells.

I'm not sure if they really expected me to dive in, but I grabbed the mask and entered the water. While I think they didn't expect me to be successful, I was just stubborn enough to prove them wrong. While I was a fairly good swimmer, I was not much of a diver. Even I didn't expect to be successful in retrieving the shell in twelve feet of water. As I got to the bottom with lungs ready to burst as a result of years of being hooked on tobacco, I thought, why had I had been so stubborn? Luckily I spotted my objective right away, grabbed it and hurried to the surface. It was worth it to see the look on Jack and Gregg's faces as I handed Jack the conch like I had been diving in twelve feet of water all my life. Amazing what a large ego can drive some people to do.

In the meantime Captain John decided that the conch shell innards might make a good snack. He cut the meat into small pieces and fried them in butter and a little lemon juice. The butter and lemon juice were tasty, the conch meat tough and chewy. Jack suggested that we take some of the chewy morsels and use them for fishing bait. Out came the fishing poles and soon we were catching small six-inch fish with a bright blue marking on the sides. I had brought a small fish guide-book along since I was aware that some tropical fish were poisonous. Unfortunately, the fish guide-book did not include the fish we were catching. We had a good time fishing. Alas, no fish were consumed.

That evening Captain John decided we should depart in the morning. After an evening of sharing, probably what were unnecessary, two hour watches we attempted to weigh the Danforth anchor, but to no avail. The anchor was solidly stuck on something. Jack and Greg came fore-ward and began to tug mercilessly on the anchor line to the degree where the bow sank downward. Finally, the anchor broke loose and up came the Danforth with a severely bent fluke and we were off to Fort Lauderdale.

Again the crossing was uneventful, with one exception. Half way across the Gulf Stream directly ahead was what I came to know as a "square grouper". "Hey John, let's get a boat hook and retrieve that thing." I shouted. "Not on your life," responded John. "That's a bail of marijuana. All we need to do is pick it up and get searched by the Coast Guard. I'd lose my boat." I sure couldn't argue with Captain John. After all, it was his boat. Drug runners would wrap marijuana in cubic bales of waterproof packets. Upon occasion these "square groupers" would be thrown overboard if the drug runners thought that they had been spotted by the authorities. Apparently this bale was thrown overboard into the north flowing Gulf Stream to the south of our course line.

Shortly thereafter we docked again at Fort Liquordale. While my exposure to the Bahamas was limited to Cat Cay, at least I had the opportunity to cross the Gulf Stream. Also, I learned how difficult it was to sail on someone else's boat and keep your mouth shut regarding the Captain's decisions. I enjoyed the experience, but couldn't wait to get back to the Great Lakes as captain of my own boat.

Things Don't Always Go Well

Jennifer Saves the Day:

Fortunately, in over thirty-five years of sailing on the Great Lakes, I have only had to be towed in twice. The first time Carol and my two daughters, Jennifer and Glenda were aboard the *Escape III*. I don't remember why, but my engine wouldn't start. I was just outside of Chagrin Lagoons and I radioed the club for a tow. My call was answered by one of the sailors who was a little tipsy from too much partying. He came out and a towing line was attached.

One of the ways a boat is stopped is by reversing the engine as the dock is approached. One year one of the sailors came in too fast and when he put his engine in reverse, it stalled and crash, an expensive bow repair. Being towed, I had no control of the speed especially reverse to slow down. On the way in the towing vessel was moving too fast. Going up a narrow channel, I had nowhere to go except into my dock slip. Otherwise I would crash into another boat.

Noting that we were moving too fast, I elected to suffer the consequence of turning into my slip and crashing into the concrete spit. As I turned in the dock slip, Jennifer tossed a line around one of the dock posts and brought us to an abrupt, undamaged halt. I marvel to this day how a twelve year old had the presence of mind to accomplish such a feat. Thank God she takes after her mother.

The *Mistress* Takes on Water:

Every new boat has to have its kinks worked out. The *Mistress* was no exception. With the advantage of an engine a sail take down is relatively easy. The craft is brought into the wind to release pressure on the sails and the sails can be dropped and furled. One day after a pleasant afternoon sail with Carol and the two girls the engine was started. I went up on deck to fold the main sail while Jennifer was at the helm. Jennifer knew to bring *Mistress* into the wind. *Mistress* was not responding. "Giver more power," I yelled at Jennifer. "I am Dad, but nothing seems to happen." I jumped back into the cockpit, revved the engine and sure enough, nothing happened. I opened the sail locker and looked down into the engine compartment. For some reason the propeller shaft had separated from the engine and slid back allowing water to come in through the resulting hole (shaft log).

We were being blown toward a stone abutment, that projects out from the adjacent electrical power plant. The first thing to be done was to raise the sails and get away from the wall. After this, it was necessary to plug the hole in the shaft log, which was accomplished by stuffing a rag in the hole. Glenda was scared and in tears. I had to do something to ease her fear and gave her the job of pumping the hand bilge pump.

I got on the radio and called for a tow. This time Helmut came out in his Tartan and slowly and safely towed me into the travel lift area. *Mistress* had to be pulled out of the water. I called Tartan and immediately they sent a repairman to access the problem. Where the prop shaft inserts into the engine, the shaft is dimpled and set-screws fit into the dimples and are safety wired. Apparently, someone forgot to dimple the shaft. It was nice to have the Tartan production facility nearby. The Tartan factory responded immediately to a call and had an employee at Chagrin Lagoons the next day.

A Life Threatening Event:

Being overtaken by a storm, running aground, or being run down by a freighter, any of these might potentially result in disaster. The most dangerous event that occurred

160

during the thirty years of sailing the *Mistress* was in no way the fault of poor seamanship or a defect in the *Mistress.*

Mr. Singer and I decided to make one last crossing of Lake Erie to Port Stanley. We made the sail there and back with an expected alternating clear and overcast sky, light rain and wind ranging from fifteen to forty knots, typical of variations in Great Lakes weather.

Shortly thereafter, it came to the sad time for haul out. Several steps are required to winterize a boat such as emptying and winterizing the fresh water tanks, removing the sails,  filling the fuel tank to prevent moisture condensation, removing the compasses and electronics, removing water from the exhaust system. During and after some of these steps are completed, a travel lift set of slings are placed under the boat. The boat is lifted out of the water and transported to and deposited on a cradle or what are called jack-stands until re-deposited in the water the following spring.

As *Mistress* was lifted out of the water, Mr. Singer and I were surprised and shocked to see what was a one-foot area that had been ground into the bottom of the hull. The remaining portion of the ground out area was paper thin. If this thin area had given way especially when we were in the middle of Lake Erie we would have possibly died or, if rescued, would probably never have known the cause of the sinking.

Among one of the actions to be taken when a vessel is taking on water is to use a bilge pump. This would not have worked since, judging from the potential size of the hole, the pump would not have kept up with the amount of water coming in. A second possibility would be to wrap a sail around and under the hull to try and seal the hole from the inflow of water. This would have been extremely difficult since the hole was behind the fuel tank and the location could not be easily identified. Fortunately for us, the hole did not break through.

Mr. Singer feeling depth of damage

The next objective was to determine what caused the hole. The lake level can vary considerably from season to season, as well as from year to year. The level can even vary within a short time span due to shifting prolonged wind across the lake surface. The lake level is lower toward the end of the summer in addition to sometimes being generally at a lower annual level. In this particular instance, the combination of factors affecting the level slowly lowered the *Mistress* onto a steel post, which in years past had been cut off below the water surface. As a result, the post served as an imperceptible grinding tool over the course of the summer.

The culprit steel pole visable as lake level subsides.

Mistress was immediately transported to the nearby Tartan factory where the repair was made over the winter season in time for the following spring,

162

Deliveries and Assistance

Mr. Singer and I had developed enough of a reputation that we were sometimes asked to deliver or help deliver the vessels of others. The following are some examples.

The Automotive Engineer:

Ted was an older gentleman with whom Mr. Singer and I would occasionally sail on Ted's boat, a 30 foot Tartan named *Snow Queen*. One time when we had sailed on *Snow Queen*, the engine wouldn't start. Ace mechanic Mr. Singer worked on the engine to no avail. I said to Ted, "You're an automotive engineer. What do you think the problem is?" Ted looked at me, somewhat taken aback, and said, "Yes, I have a degree in automotive engineering and I can tell you all about theory of engines, but don't ask me to work on or how to fix an engine." With constant tinkering, Mr. Singer was finally successful at starting the engine, but was not sure why. Ted said he would have to have a mechanic look at his engine.

Later that month, Ted had sailed *Snow Queen* to Catawba Island with some friends, and met some others. He decided to return to Cleveland by auto leaving his boat behind at a friend's private dock. He asked if Mr. Singer and I could return it to his Cleveland yacht club. Sure, why not?

Ted drove us to Catawba Island to drop us off. Catawba Island is located in the group of islands in the southwest portion of Lake Erie approximately sixty-five miles due west of Cleveland. Catawba Island originally was an island but is now connected to the mainland and consequently, is actually a peninsula.

We departed at 1130 with virtually no wind. We continued under power toward Cleveland. All seemed to be going well until 1630 off of Lorain the engine quit. Mr. Singer went below and, as he had done previously, tinkered with the engine. Finally, he came up and said, "I've done everything I can think of." If Mr. Singer couldn't fix it, while under way with the tools and parts available, then no one could fix it. We'd just have to make the best of it in extremely light air. Wouldn't you know it? Just when we needed a storm or at least heavier winds, fickle Lake Erie had us nearly becalmed?

Slowly, with what little wind (1 to 4 knots) was coming out of the southwest, we attempted to catch any whisper of wind. Mr. Singer would, from time to time, go below and tinker with the engine a little more, but again to no avail. "Give up Mr. Singer. You've done all you can under the circumstances." And so he did and we continued almost imperceptibly making our way toward Cleveland.

We reached the main entrance to Cleveland Harbor at half past midnight. As we headed toward the harbor entrance, a large freighter was coming out of the Cuyahoga River mouth. Since the freighter had the right of way, we slowly turned northeast away from the harbor entrance to avoid the freighter. As the several hundred foot long freighter cleared the entrance we again turned toward the harbor entrance passing between the east and west break-walls.*

---

* Initially, sailboats (not under power) had the right of way since mechanically powered vessels were more maneuverable. In later years, this rule rightfully was altered since larger vessels often are not more maneuverable, especially within confined channels.

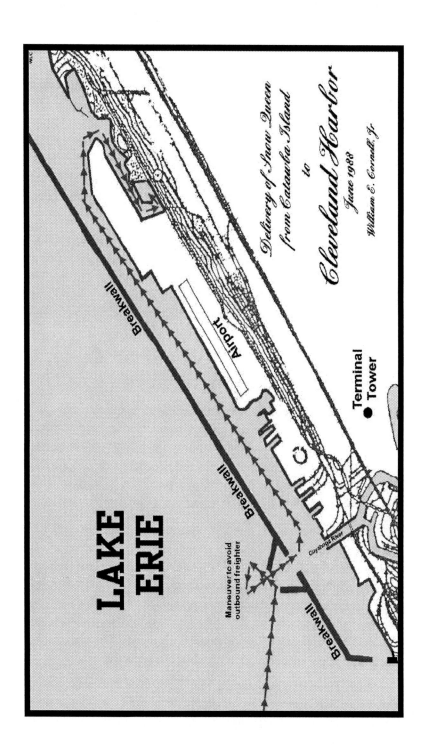

Delivery of Snow Queen
from Catawba Island
to
Cleveland Harbor
June 1988
William E. Cevrell, Jr.

LAKE ERIE

Breakwall

Breakwall

Breakwall

Airport

Terminal Tower

Guyahoga River

Maneuver to avoid outbound freighter

It was an hour before we were again able to make our way into the harbor entrance and entered between the east and west break walls. We again slowly turned northeast and continued to make our way along the inside of the break wall before turning into a narrow southwest channel leading to Ted's yacht club. As we were making our way in this channel a Coast Guard vessel was heading out to tow a boat in. As they passed, one of the crew yelled out, "We'll be back to give you a tow as soon as we pull in a powerboat."

Shortly thereafter, they came by with the tow. After safely delivering the powerboat, they returned and offered to give us a tow. I responded, "Naw. We've been doing this for almost twelve hours and it's now a challenge to make it the last few hundred yards, but thanks anyway." Mr. Singer wholeheartedly agreed. We finally docked at 0400.

A Leaky Boat:

Someone told Mr. Singer and I about a fellow, I'll call him Irwin, whose wife didn't particularly care for sailing. Irwin thought that maybe he could get her to enjoy some relatively short romantic sails in the protected waters of the North Channel. The only problem Irwin had was his thirty-nine foot, center cockpit C & C was in Cleveland.

Irwin, we were told, needed someone to help him get his boat to North Channel. We were always looking for an opportunity to experience other boats. We were led to believe that Irwin was an excellent sailor and Mr. Singer and I decided to investigate this possibility further. One day we met Irwin at his boat and before committing ourselves, wanted to inspect the boat and equipment. The boat was well equipped with the items that came with the boat.

I told Irwin that we would help him take the boat north, but there were a few items such as a radar reflector and safety harnesses, which he would have to purchase before we would agree to sail with him. Irwin reluctantly agreed and we set a date for departure.

On the afternoon of departure there was little wind as we headed for the Peelee Passage about fifty miles to the northwest. Lake Erie was in one of its moods again and the windless day turned into a windless evening as we sat around talking. Since this would be an all nighter, I decided to go below and get some shut-eye.

About 0200 Mr. Singer shook my arm and said, "Hey Corn, I think we're in trouble." "Why? What's the matter?" "While examining a chart, a bilge board just floated up against my foot." With that pronouncement, I scampered up and sure enough the cabin sole was awash with water. We were still under power with Irwin at the helm as I pulled up the floorboards. Nothing but sloshing water. We then opened the engine compartment to see the engine chugging away despite being half under water. I noticed a gurgling sound coming from the engine and thought I had found where the water was coming in. I felt around the where the gurgling sound was emanating, but it didn't feel like any water was coming in. I asked, "Irwin is the electric bilge pump on?" "Yes, I've had it on for a while, he said. "Mr. Singer, try the hand bilge pump," I commanded." "I did, but it doesn't to work." "O.K. then, lets get a bucket brigade going and see if we can bail out the water. Irwin, take her out of gear, but don't shut down the engine. I'll bail out of the engine compartment, Mr. Singer hand up the bucket to Irwin and let's see if we can make any progress."

Slowly the water level went down. More importantly, it stayed down. We spent the next week trying to solve the mystery. Where did the water come in and why did it stop? During the next few days, the bilge was checked with great regularity.

We could hear the sound of the electric bilge pump, but why didn't the hand bilge pump work? Mr. Singer and I had to figure it out in case there was another inexplicable water mystery. Oddly, the end of the hand bilge pump hose ran all the way to the interior stern. Mr. Singer crawled into the stern behind the engine compartment. He couldn't get to the end of the hose since it was stapled in place. He had to rip the hose out to get to the end. The end of the hose had a screen, which was clogged with sawdust, wood chips, and fiberglass debris accumulated when the vessel was built. We cleaned this and rerouted the hose into an easily accessible section of the bilge in the main cabin.

We continued our journey to the mouth of the Detroit River, up the river past Detroit, across Lake St. Clair and up the St. Clair River to Port Huron on the Michigan side of the River. We then departed Port Huron, under the Blue Water Bridge and on to Lake Huron. The only significant negative aspect of the journey was listening to Irwin complain about the cost of purchasing the equipment, especially the radar reflector, which I had insisted that Irwin acquire before we were willing to sail north with him.

It should be noted that the routes of both up-bound and down-bound freighters converge at the entrance to the St. Clair River. As a result, freighter traffic intensifies in the southern portion of Lake Huron. While in this section of Lake Huron a dense fog set in. The horns of several freighters now called out around us. I never again heard a comment from Irwin about purchasing the radar reflector or other equipment.

Mr. Singer had to depart from the voyage and was able to meet his parents in Michigan for return to Cleveland. Shortly thereafter we departed U.S. waters and entered the North Channel. We had still not figured why water had filled the bilge, but was no longer doing so. Then a possibility came to mind. "Hey Irwin, did you ever do any work on the electric bilge pump?" "No, but a friend of mine did pull out the bilge pump motor when it wasn't running and fixed it. It's O.K. though, he knows a lot about boats."

I then poured a couple of buckets of water into the bilge and turned on the pump. Nothing happened except a slight gurgling in the bilge. I then disconnected the bilge pump and reversed the two connections. Switch on and the bilge emptied.

Why did this occur intermittently? The electric bilge pump hose was located and emptied low on the transom. When Irwin's boat was under power, the stern would squat placing the electric bilge pump hose outlet below the water line. When under power, if the electric bilge pump was turned on, water would be pumped into the bilge; when under sail the pump would only pump air, thus, explaining the intermittent presence of water in the bilge.

When I had completed my obligation to help Irwin get his boat to the North Channel I was to fly back to Cleveland. Irwin had made arrangements with a pilot friend to bring his wife and some friends for some cruising in the North Channel. I was to fly on the return trip to Cleveland.

I never did find out if Irwin was to achieve his short romantic sail in the protected waters of the North Channel. Once again, I was ready to get back to sailing the *Mistress*.

The Delivery

Interruption:

In March of 2002 my sailing experience was seriously curtailed. While on a business trip to New Orleans I began to feel exceptionally week. Upon my return to Cleveland, I could barely make it through the Cleveland Hopkins Airport without sitting down to rest several times. I finally made it to my automobile and home. When I struggled through the door, I told my wife Carol "Something is really wrong. I better go to a doctor as soon as possible."

The next day I went to the doctor's office where a nurse drew blood for testing. She told me she would call me with the results sometime the following day. I told her that I had a business meeting in Youngstown the next day, but leave a message. I returned home, turned on the television, and stretched out on the couch. Later that same evening I received a call from the nurse who said "You're not going to Youngstown tomorrow. Instead you're going right to the hospital in the morning."

I went to the hospital, went through a series of tests and after a week was told by a doctor, "Well, Mr. Cornell, I have some bad news and some good news." "What's the bad news?" I responded. "You have acute myeloma leukemia referred to as AML." In a state of shock, I asked, "What's the good news?" You're only twenty minutes from the best place in the world for treatment, the Cleveland Clinic."

I was then transferred and began a series of in-hospital chemotherapy treatments. In the meantime, Mr. Singer was in Hawaii taking care of his elderly parents. After thirty-two days of hospitalization, I finally was discharged, but had to take additional chemotherapy treatments. When Mr. Singer temporarily returned from Hawaii we finally launched *Mistress* in June before he had to return to Hawaii. Needles to say *Mistress* remained docked during the 2002 season as I continued my chemotherapy treatments.

During the next few years sailing the *Mistress* was seriously curtailed except for occasional short sojourns to Port Stanley, Ontario and the Lake Erie Islands. I was further handicapped by having a fungal lung infection. This required steroids and various injections of medication delivered through what is called a Hickman device. The Hickman device connected to a vein in my neck to permit a daily injection of medication.

Not being one to sit around for four hours while the medication was passing through the Hickman. I would put the medication bag over my auto rear view mirror and continue on my way. One year I sailed with a friend Bill Burrows in his 27 foot wood Hershoff designed sailboat to the All Wood Classics Weekend at the Huron, Ohio boat basin. Several attending sailors were shocked, entertained, amused and awestruck when I hung my medication on a hand hold and hooked up to my Hickman.

One of the results of the steroid use was the rapid development (they call it ripening) of cataracts. On one occasion when Mr. Singer and I were returning to our homeport at night, I realized I could no longer see navigation lights. My vision was declining so rapidly that I finally told Mr. Singer that I could no longer sail at night.

Fortunately, since the steroid use had discontinued, I was able to have an operation wherein a lens was replaced. When the eye cover was removed in preparation for the doctor's examination, I panicked. A wall in the room had previously appeared cream colored, it now appeared a bluish white. The reason I panicked was now I had double vision. When the doctor came in, I told her about the double vision. She assured me that the double vision was from having one eye covered, my vision would return to normal shortly. She was right.

While testing the vision of the operated eye, I told her that I had utilized contact lenses for several years with what was called mono-vision. Mono-vision is when one eye is corrected for distance vision while the other eye is corrected for reading. When my earliest dock partner Elwood (Bull) Sawitke, an optometrist, told me about mono-vision I thought he had lost it. He promised me that if I would try it, he guaranteed I'd be satisfied or there would be no cost. I tried it and sure enough, it worked. This was a tremendous advantage to me in that the type of work I did required me to find locations while driving and constantly refer to a map.

The doctor said, "Sure, we can do that." Shortly thereafter the second operation was performed and now I can see close and at a distance. At least something good, besides being alive, resulted from this potentially tragic experience.

Within two years of my original diagnosis I felt it was time to more intensely resume my sailing activity.

Return to Sailing:

A few years earlier Mr. Singer had decided to study for a U.S. Coast Guard captain's license. He wanted me to attempt to also secure the license. At the time, I was unable to take the necessary time since I was working more than fourteen hours a day, seven days a week in the winter and six days a week in the summer. Hell, I hardly had time to take care of the *Mistress* or take an occasional day trip.

Suddenly, because of the maladies mentioned and the resulting forced retirement, I found myself with a plethora of time and a fuzzy mind. Fuzzy was the only way I can describe my mind functioning. Despite this fuzziness, I guess from the chemotherapy treatments, Mr. Singer convinced me to study for the captain's license. Not only did he convince me to study for the Coast Guard license, but also spent day after day at my dining room table going over the materials. I was able to finally outline my required boating experience and pass the examination. Then Mr. Singer accompanied me to the Coast Guard office in Toledo, Ohio. I was able to pass some additional examinations wherein I was able to add endorsements to my license for towing and sailing.

Mr. Singer and I then decided we were a perfect pair to deliver boats. After all, Mr. Singer had delivered a boat from Florida to Louisiana, sailed the Florida west coast a number of times with his father in law; I had sailed the Caribbean, to the Bahamas and to the Dry Tortugas; we had helped deliver a 39 foot CC center cockpit to the North Channel, and sailed the Great Lakes for a number of years. Now, to find a job professionally delivering someone's boat.

In the Spring of 2005, I was preparing *Mistress* after the winter lay-up. A friend George Raynor had sold his boat *Hardtack*, a 27 foot Tartan, to a young fellow from Racine, Wisconsin. *Hardtack*, despite being over forty years old, and George had become somewhat of a legend on Lake Erie. George, an avid racing sailor, had won numerous races in *Hardtack*. One of these was called the Falcon Cup that ran about 26 nautical miles (30 statute miles) from the Cleveland Yacht Club at Rocky River, Ohio (the west side of Metropolitan Cleveland) to the Mentor Yacht Club at Mentor, Ohio (the east side of Metropolitan Cleveland). Despite the fact that several competitors had larger expensive boats, *Hardtack* on numerous occasions, much to the dismay of many racing sailors, would take the Falcon Cup. Those around George, including non-racing sailors and even power boaters, got a real kick out of George and his forty-plus year old Tartan, almost consistently winning the Falcon Cup.

One day while getting *Mistress* ready for launching, I ran into the fellow by name of David who had bought the *Hardtack* from George. David was from Racine, Wisconsin. I questioned what were his plans for getting the *Hardtack*, which was sitting on land nearby, to Racine. David responded, "I'm not sure yet. I may sail her a few week-end days, somehow return to Racine and get back the following week-end until I finally get her back to Racine. I may be able to get some friends to pick me up at various times."

With that, I pulled out one of my business cards, "Corsin Yacht Delivery" gave it to Dave and told him that Mr. Singer and I could deliver *Hardtack* to Racine and save him considerable time and expense. Dave took the card and said, "I'll think it over." In the meantime Dave launched the *Hardtack* and took her for a couple short sails. Dave also did his due diligence and questioned around to determine if we were competent for the delivery.

Mr. Singer and I were known for our unusual marathon sails in terms of time and distances. Also we were known to often depart at night in fairly inclement weather, not that we were reckless, but reasonably confident. After questioning around, Dave decided he would take a chance. After all what did he have to lose besides an aged sailboat.

Cleveland from off shore.

Soon Mr. Singer again returned from Hawaii. David, Mr. Singer and I were busy getting *Hardtack* ready for the trip. David had bought and installed an electric self-steering device. (This quit working once we got to Lake Huron.) Mr. Singer and I checked the sails, rigging, and navigation lights. I had the necessary charts of Lakes Erie, Huron, St. Clair, and the Detroit and St Clair Rivers, but not Lake Michigan and its ports. Before returning to Racine, David promised to ship us the necessary Lake Michigan charts. Fortunately, these arrived shortly before our departure. We also had the task of purchasing food, miscellaneous items such as food preparation utensils, flash-lights, batteries, etc. We also acquired and filled two large 20- gallon jerry tanks with gasoline. We would leave these with *Hardtack* after delivery. Finally, Mr. Singer rigged up a small light over a makeshift navigation table.

We departed at 0530 with fair weather. After passing Cleveland barely visible to the south and making our way through the Pelee Passage we arrived at the mouth of the Detroit River at midnight.

Navigating the Detroit River, especially at night, is a daunting task. There are numerous navigation lights easily confused with what is known as "back-scatter". Also some of the shipping channels,

Down bound freighter in the Pelee Passage

while dredged to a 28 foot depth, often border adjacent areas as shallow as 2 feet. Ever since I have been sailing and as many times as I have transited the Detroit River, I've marveled at how large freighters can thread their way through these relatively narrow channels.

One of the problems we ran into on the way up the Detroit River at night was that our steamer light was not working. (A sailboat when under power must show the same lighting as a power-boat.) Since we were under power at night, we had to jerry-rig one of our flashlights and tape it to the forward part of the mast. Necessity is the mother of invention.

Slowly we proceeded to make our way past the large industrial, mostly steel plants, on the American side of the river, past Henry Ford's complex at the River Rouge. By the break of dawn we approached Detroit skyline and the Ambassador Bridge, which crosses from Detroit to Windsor, Ontario.

As the sky brightened we crossed the well-marked channel of Lake St. Clair to the mouth of the more easily navigable St. Clair River. Over the last few years I had noticed a continuing discernable

Ore freighter against early morning Detroit skyline upbound on the Detroit River.

decrease of shipping traffic on numerous voyages on the Great Lakes including the Detroit and St. Clair Rivers. There was still lake and international shipping, but substantially reduced.

While motoring up the St. Clair River we agreed that it was time to check the fuel before we ran out. *Hardtack*'s fuel tank fill cap was centrally located on the cockpit sole. Ever since the fuel incident aboard the *Escape III*, I've always been wary regarding boats and gasoline. Every now and then you'd hear of some boat blowing up due to carelessness. While at the edge of the river we shut down the engine, ran the blower and removed the fill cap. *Hardtack* had an interesting fuel gauge arrangement. This consisted of a narrow length of wood, which was inserted into the fill hole to determine how much fuel remained. This we did and agreed it was time to use one of the jerry cans.

All went well, but we knew we had to get additional fuel. We pulled into a small inlet (the mouth of the Belle River) located at a town called Marine City. We waited for someone to approach us for fuel. "Mr. Singer, think anyone is around?" "You better walk up to the office," responded Mr. Singer. I walked up to the office and was greeted by the clerk or owner who was very laid back. "Can I hep you?" "Yes, we need to fuel up." "Just leave your credit card here and go ahead." I went back to *Hardtack,* told Mr. Singer to make sure all switches were off, and close up the *Hardtack.*

Russian freighter upbound in the St. Clair River

When finished another boat pulled in. Mr. Singer assisted them with docking while I opened the *Hardtack* for ventilation and ran the blower for an adequate amount of time. When I returned to the office to finalize the transaction, the other boat captain went with me to leave his credit card. We went back to the fuel dock and I told Mr. Singer, "Get ready to cast off." As we were leaving the recently arrived captain grabbed the fuel hose and immediately began to fuel his vessel with out taking the necessary pre-fueling precautions. "Let's get out of here before that idiot blows us up." As we swung back into the St. Clair River, I said, "No wonder someone blows themselves up every now and then."

By that evening we were passing Port Huron, Michigan and about to go under the Bluewater Bridge, the last vehicle crossing from Michigan to Ontario. Here, as mentioned earlier, is one of the strongest navigable currents on the Great Lakes. All the water from the upper Great Lakes is funneling into the St. Clair River. Mr. Singer and I had passed this way several times before in the *Mistress* with a forty hp engine. How would the *Hardtack* handle this current with a smaller engine? As we hugged the Canadian shore we revved the engine to a full r.p.m. and slowly were able to enter Lake Huron at dusk.

We sailed/motored, depending on the wind, for the night, next day and night and next day finally pulling into Rogers City, Michigan at 2000 after three and one-half days and approximately 380 statute miles (330 nautical miles). For the most part so far the trip had been uneventful except for the steamer light episode on the Detroit River and to our dismay, on the last segment of the trip northward on Lake Huron when the automatic helm would no longer function. Obviously, one of us would have to continuously man the helm when under way for the remainder of the delivery.

Rogers City had a well-protected harbor operated by some college kids for the State of Michigan. Once we were tied up, a thirty-two foot power-boat came in and docked next to us. Mr. Singer hopped onto the dock and took some lines to assist this lone captain, helped tie him up and returned to the *Hardtack*. This captain had several fishing rigs on board and was obviously an avid fisherman. "You guys want some salmon?" he queried. "Sure," was our response in unison. With that, he passed a large slab of fresh caught salmon, closed up his boat and was off to his parked automobile.

Mr. Singer and I looked questioningly at each other. We had not prepared for this. Our desire for food had been simplified to canned stew or boiled whatever. "Corn, what'ya think we should do with this?" "I don't know, but maybe we could put it into the frying pan. If only we had some lemon and butter." "Good idea. Let's see if we can find a grocery store." We wondered up to the marina office and Mr. Singer asked "Is there a grocery store around?" "Yes", responded one of the kids. "Come on. I'll drive you there."

We wandered through the local store and secured ice, some fresh provisions including butter and a bottle of concentrated lemon juice. When we returned to the marina we wanted to give the kid something for his trouble. "Naw" he said, "just part of my job."

Maybe it was because we had eaten nothing except crackers, potato chips, canned and boiled food for the last couple of days, but fresh salmon heated briefly in a frying pan and marinated with butter and lemon juice was one of the better meals I have ever consumed.

That night, after gorging ourselves, we soon collapsed or perhaps I should say passed out until the next morning. We were not particularly anxious to get underway and slowly straightened and cleaned *Hardtack*. The fisherman dock partner was on his boat. "You guys sleep alright last night?" "We slept just fine and thoroughly enjoyed the salmon." piped up Mr. Singer. "I thought you guys would be gone by now. Here's a couple more slabs of salmon. Hell, I'll never eat it all." We stowed this gastric windfall, which we consumed over the next two evening meals. We cast off at 1000 heading for the Straits of Mackinac approximately fifty-five miles to the northeast and on to Lake Michigan.

We determined that we could pass under the Mackinac Bridge and on to Lake Michigan before darkness. By the early evening we passed Mackinac Island with its famous Grand Hotel. The Grand Hotel, constructed in 1887, supports the largest porch in the world. I had sailed to Mackinac Island several years previously. I would have liked to have enjoyed the many amenities of this Victorian era atmosphere (automobiles are not permitted on the island) but, alas Mr. Singer and I had a delivery to complete.

In the remaining hours of daylight we approached and passed under the bridge. The Mackinac Bridge is a four-lane structure (I-75) connecting the two Michigan peninsulas and, opened in 1957. At a length of over five miles, it is one of the largest bridges in the world. The roadway is a steel grid, which permits one, when passing below, to see traffic crossing. The steel grid permits the flow of air and permits stability, unlike the famous wind waving destruction of the Tacoma Narrows suspension bridge in 1940.

Moving west under the Mackinac Bridge

We began to make our way southwest. Darkness set in and we soon had an unseen Beaver Island a few miles to the west. Mr. Singer had spent numerous summers in this northwest area of the lower-peninsula and began conversing about some recollections of his memory of Beaver Island. He indicated that at one time he thought Beaver Island had declared itself an independent country. Mr. Singer's memory was somewhat obscured by forty years. Actually, Beaver Island was settled by an off-shoot of Mormons led by a gentleman named James Strang. Strang declared himself king and named his capital St. James, named after himself of course. Shortly thereafter, Strang was murdered, the Mormon community moved away, and Beaver Island was then settled mainly by Irish.

As we continued on a south, southwest course shortly after dawn the wind began to build out of the southwest. Sails came down and we began to power into eight- foot waves. Not being able to make significant way toward our destination and having sailed for two days, we decided to put into port until the wind turned more favorable. Mr. Singer initially suggested Charlevoix a port he was familiar with from forty years ago. I went below to check our position and found Charlevoix to be to the northeast. Rather than losing distance, after Mr. Singer went below to double check our position (as mentioned previously we always double checked our position), it was decided we would continue pounding into the waves and attempt to get to Leland about fifteen miles to the south.

By dusk we entered the harbor at Leland (population 2,000) and docked. The wind was continuing out of the southwest at thirty knots. "What'll you want to do Mr. Singer?" "I think we should find a bar, have a couple of drinks and a meal." replied Mr. Singer. "Good idea." since we now had finished our salmon. Off we went to the nearest bar, after which, back to the *Hardtack* for a sound nights sleep.

The next morning we slept in until almost noon. As the day wore on, a strong wind continued blowing out of the southwest.

Hardtack at Leland Michigan

We spent the day conversing with other sailors while waiting for the wind to ameliorate, either in intensity or direction. "What do you think about staying in Leland for another night? After all, the wind will be right on the nose and we certainly won't be able to make much headway." I opined to Mr. Singer. "Guess you're right Corn. Besides, we could use the rest."

Sometime during the night the wind settled down and we departed Leland heading along the shore and eventually to the southwest diagonally across Lake Michigan. Mr. Singer was thoroughly enjoying himself reminiscing about his adventures as a kid especially, when we were passing the Sleeping Dunes National Lakeshore.

By now the wind had died off and we made our way through the remainder of the day and all night. As the west shore of Lake Michigan slowly came into view, we decided to put into Sheboygan, WI. With little wind we had been mainly under power for the last 140 miles. At this point a fuel stop was mandatory. We pulled into the harbor and up to the fuel pumps just after daybreak. The area was deserted except for a few nearby, local sport fishermen who were cleaning their night's catch at a public cleaning table.

After refueling, I went below to check the chart. "Mr. Singer, looks like we have about seventy-five more miles to reach Racine." "Well, let's get going," Mr. Singer replied. With that we departed south somewhat paralleling the shoreline that was receding slightly to the west. By the time we reached Milwaukee we were ten miles off shore. At his point the shoreline begins to gradually swing to the east culminating with a projection called Wind Point located about four miles north-northeast of Racine. Just before reaching Wind Point I called David via cell phone to let him know that we expected to arrive that evening. "Be careful of Wind Point," cautioned David. "Yeah, we see it. We'll call you when we're docked."

It almost seemed easier to get to Racine than it did getting into Racine. By the time we reached the entrance to the harbor it was dark and the back-scatter of shore lights contributed to the confusion of identifying the brake wall and other navigation lights. For a while we zigzagged outside the entrance to the harbor until we could finally make our way beyond the brake wall. Once inside the harbor confusion continued. Straight ahead was a marked channel up the Root River (Racine is French for root) while another channel to the right led to numerous docked boats. We elected to take the channel to the right and tied up at a long vacant wharf leading from a clubhouse. It was after 2200.

I called David to announce our arrival and soon David met us. We had a drink to celebrate our safe and timely arrival. We briefly described our journey and outlined various items that were defective, missing or just not working. These were later outlined in a Corsin Yacht Delivery Synopsis and Notes sent to David soon after our return to Ohio.

David said he had to work the next day, but would see us shortly after work. That gave us time to look around the nearby downtown area. Many years earlier I had worked in the Racine area trying to relocate a Firestone store. The city had condemned the existing store location and Firestone, through my efforts, was able to purchase and build a new facility on the edge of the downtown area. I was anxious to see if the store was still there. It was.

The end of the journey
Racine Yacht Club
June 27, 2005

Later that day David came back to the *Hardtack*. He told us that he had investigated a means for our return to Ohio. We could take a train from Racine to Chicago and there transfer to an Amtrak train that would arrive in Cleveland around 0300. The next day he drove us to the Racine station and dropped us off for our return to Cleveland.

Mr. Singer and I were well satisfied with our performance. We had safely delivered *Hardtack* as paid professional captains a distance of almost 800 miles in eight and one-half days.

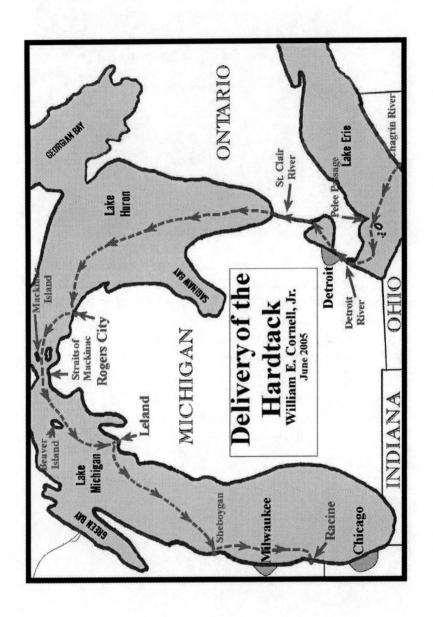

Delivery of the Hardtack
William E. Cornell, Jr.
June 2005

Anchoring

Since many voyages are often concluded with an anchorage, I thought it appropriate to end this writing endeavor with the subject of some anchoring (often referred to as "dropping the hook") experiences.

There are many joys to experiencing the comradeship of fellow sailors; the comforts and pleasures of various towns, yacht clubs and marinas; the challenges and satisfaction of successful navigation; the exhilaration of riding out a storm; and the discovery of unknown areas. Successfully anchoring, in a well-protected area, stands alone as a respite from the intensity of the above experiences.

Anchors come in all different sizes and shapes. Different types of anchors have been developed for different kinds of bottoms i.e. sandy, muddy, rocky, grassy. My first anchoring experience was when I went for the bareboat instruction with Captain Deutschman in Long Island Sound. Captain Deutschman explained that anchoring involved more than just tossing the anchor over the side. Before letting the anchor go the vessel should first be headed into the wind. An anchor works not by its weight, but rather by digging into the bottom. In order for this to be accomplished enough line (scope) is to be let out depending on the depth of the water to create an angle so that the anchor can dig into the bottom. Once the anchor is on the bottom with enough scope, the vessel will slowly settle downwind and drag the anchor as it digs into the bottom.*

---

* Upon occasion, if necessary, the engine can be run in reverse for a short time to get the anchor to dig in to the bottom (set).

The first time I anchored on my own was when I went to the British Virgins. (*A Virgin Experience*) The water in the Caribbean is perfect for the inexperienced yachtsman due to its clarity. When the anchor was dropped and the boat powered in reverse to set the anchor, I could swim out over the anchor and see that it was securely dug in. The anchor was set each night during this trip with no problem.

The One That Got Away:

Anchoring in the Great Lakes is a different proposition. As with anchoring anywhere, especially on a long-term basis, the anchoring site should be in a protected area. When anchoring at night, for some reason, I seemed to awaken fairly often and check to make sure the anchor is secure, the wind hasn't shifted, and other boats, if anchored nearby, aren't loose or swinging toward me. One night I was anchored at Mackinaw Island and a boat came loose from its anchorage and began to drift toward other boats. Fortunately, someone had spotted this and began to yell toward the drifting boat. Someone got into a dinghy to try to fend off this drifting boat with a dragging anchor. The surprised owner was finally awakened, staggered from below and was able to start his boat and retrieve his anchor before repositioning himself and properly setting his anchor.

Anchoring in Open Water:

Occasionally a temporary anchorage can be secured in open unprotected water. One day Mr. Singer and I decided to pay a visit to Doc "Bull" Sawitke who lived in a home on lake front property. The lake was calm and the weather favorable. After anchoring in open water about 300 feet off shore, we swam to shore and sampled some of Bull's refreshments after which, we swam back to the *Mistress*. This kind of temporary anchoring should only be attempted under ideal conditions, i.e. good weather, good holding bottom and calm seas.

Put-in-Bay:

Even in ideal situations anchoring can prove to be difficult. One late evening Mr. Singer and I arrived at Put-in-bay with the intent of using a mooring ball[*] to settle in. Unbeknownst to us that year the mooring balls had been removed. Consequently, we were forced to attempt to anchor. Mr. Singer made his way to the bow to release the anchor. When in position and heading into the wind, I yelled, "Drop the anchor." Away went the anchor and I waited for the *Mistress* to settle back and the anchor to dig in. Whenever anchoring one must wait for the anchor to set and make observation of the relative position (bearings) of surrounding fixed land features such as a light, telephone pole, or point of land meeting the water.

After dropping the anchor and settling back, we took bearings and noted the anchor was dragging. "Let's try again Mr. Singer." With that I slowly eased the *Mistress* forward as Mr. Singer gathered the payed out anchor line. This proved to be a monumental task and soon we discovered the reason. As the anchor broke water, it was covered with a long stream of heavy bottom growth. (described on nautical charts as "grassy bottom"). No wonder the anchor hadn't dug in. It was merely sliding along the bottom, gathering growth as it slipped along.

I circled *Mistress* around and again into the wind for another attempt with the same results. "Hey Corn, let's try one last time." After the third unsuccessful attempt at anchoring and, by this time, due to Mr. Singer's exhaustion, it was decided to determine an alternative.

---

[*] A mooring is a line attached to semi-permanent heavy item on the bottom thence attached to a floating object. (usually a ball shape)

"Hey Corn, let's go over to near the monument and see if we can get some holding ground." "Yeah, but we'll not be very sheltered in case the wind shifts to out of the north," I said. Despite potentially not being sheltered we made our way over to the Perry Peace Memorial Monument and were successfully able to anchor. After taking bearings we rowed into the town, but kept a wary eye on the *Mistress*. Upon returning, we alternately kept a watch that evening to make sure the wind did not shift to out of the north.

Misery Bay:

Misery Bay is an anchorage surrounded by Presque Isle State Park, and within Presque Isle Bay which projects into Lake Erie from Erie, Pennsylvania. It was in Presque Isle Bay that two ships, the Lawrence and Niagara, were constructed for Oliver Hazard Perry during the War of 1812. ("Don't give up the ship") After the Battle of Lake Erie, the ships were sunk in Misery Bay because they were damaged beyond repair. Nearby, several sailors were buried.

The problem with reaching Misery Bay after entering the deep channel into Presque Isle Bay is that the depth to the northwest is shallow. After entering the Presque Isle Bay we turned to the northwest and slowly made our way toward Misery Bay hoping to not run aground. Along the west bank of the peninsula small cabin like structures on pilings jutted into the bay. Once we made it into the small bay the water depth drops to more than 10 feet. After taking our bearings, we were secure and protected enough to prepare dinner and gain a comfortable nights rest. The next day we were able to carefully exit Misery Bay without incident.

The Pool:

Through the years Mr. Singer and I experienced numerous favorable anchorages beginning with the anchorage at Quebec Harbour (*Voyage to Michipicoten Island*) and several anchorages in an area called North Channel. North Channel is that body of water that is separated from Lake Huron by Manitoulin Island (the largest fresh water island in the world). The North Channel is a yachtsmen's paradise with numerous small towns (Little Current, Gore Bay, Killarney) and innumerable secure anchorages.

Mistress at "The Pool"
Note: the *Damn Thing*

One of the most memorable anchorages was a small bay called "The Pool". This area is approximately ten miles east, northeast of the main portion of North Channel up a narrow fiord like passage called Baie Fine.

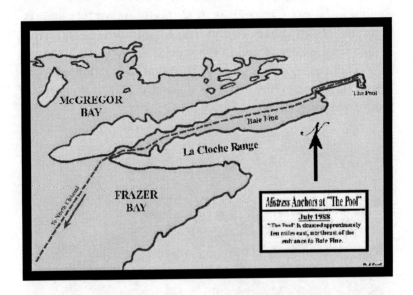

McGREGOR BAY

The Pool

Baie Fine

La Cloche Range

To North Channel

FRAZER BAY

N

Mistress Anchors at "The Pool"

July 1988

"The Pool" is situated approximately ten miles east, northeast of the entrance to Baie Fine.

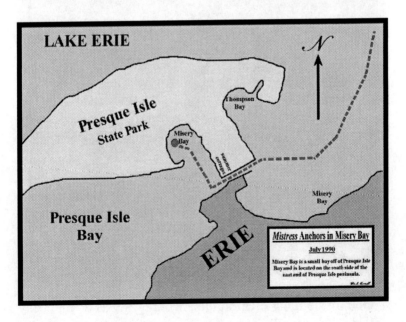

LAKE ERIE

N

Thompson Bay

Presque Isle State Park

Misery Bay

Presque Isle Bay

Misery Bay

ERIE

Mistress Anchors in Misery Bay

July 1990

Misery Bay is a small bay off of Presque Isle Bay and is located on the south side of the east end of Presque Isle peninsula.

The entrance to Baie Fine is extremely narrow (about 500 feet), but then widens to about one mile before again narrowing to a couple hundred feet for two miles and ending at the small anchorage known at "The Pool". "The Pool" has a ten-foot depth and is surrounded by a dense forest and granite outcroppings. The quiet of this desolate area was only interrupted by the occasional sound of a loon, the provincial bird of Ontario.

The Dry Tortugas:

One of the major disadvantages of sailing on the Great Lakes is the sailing season only lasts for about seven months (March to October). When a powerboat friend who lives in Florida invited me to come to Florida, I jumped at the chance. The more I thought about it, the more I thought we should charter a bare-boat and sail to the Dry Tortugas, seventy miles west of Key West. For years, for some reason, I had heard stories about the Dry Tortugas. (Dry because the only water is that captured from rain fall; Tortugas-Spanish for turtle because the island had numerous turtles)

Most people are unaware that Key West is not the end of the Florida Keys. Twenty-three miles to the west are found the Marguesas Keys and approximately forty-seven miles further to the west are found the Dry Tortugas. When I suggested to Paul that we charter a boat in Key West and sail to the Dry Tortugas, Paul agreed that this would be an interesting experience. This would be one of my most interesting anchoring experiences.

We flew in to Key West and went to pick up and provision our boat, a forty-one foot Hunter named *Bafo*. (We were to learn *Bafo* was derived from "best and final offer"). Two gals operated the charter service. "Where you going?" questioned one of the gals. "To the Dry Tortugas," I responded. "Know there's lottsa shallow water and sand banks toward the Tortugas. Why don't cha just travel around the keys? There's lots to see." I wasn't about to get into an argument and simply muttered, "Yeah, we might just try that," knowing full well I was determined to sail to the Dry Tortugas.

After a quick review of the charts we headed west for an anchorage in the Marquesas Keys. The Marquesas Keys are surrounded by very shallow water except for a deeper area to the west where we anchored for the evening. While the anchor held well all night, I was up periodically for an anchor watch as I usually do when anchoring.

The next day we were off to continue the forty-seven mile stretch sometimes accompanied by an occasional dolphin or passing a turtle. As we approached the channel leading into the anchorage area, I saw some kids walking in the water swimming along the edge of the channel. Would the channel be deep enough to get through? Is this the right entrance to the anchorage area. I didn't have Mr. Singer to double check the chart. "Take the helm Paul and circle around. I'm going to recheck the chart." This indeed was the entrance, so in we went with plenty of water. As soon as the anchor was set, we took the inflatable ashore to Fort Jefferson.

Fort Jefferson was constructed in the early 1800's to protect shipping in the Florida Straight, the area between the Florida Keys and Cuba, and to combat piracy. It was used during the Civil War to confine Confederate prisoners of war. Its most famous prisoner was Dr. Samuel Mudd who was wrongly convicted as being a part of the conspiracy in the assassination of Lincoln. Dr. Mudd was subsequently released.

We began to walk around the Fort when we came upon a man and woman. The man was putting out a cigarette when I yelled, "Hey! There's no smoking on this island." He turned toward me and when he saw a cigar in my mouth, broke out in a wide smile and said, "You picked the wrong guy to pick on." "Why's that?" "Because this is a National Park and I'm the chief ranger in charge. We all had a good laugh.

The ranger claimed to be a full blooded Sioux Indian and his wife was from Alaska. They appeared hungry for conversation and invited us to a dinner of all you could eat shrimp and lobster the next evening. Duty in the Dry Tortugas offers a limited human contact. Due to its isolation within the Gulf of Mexico and a limited ferry service from Key West, few visitors come to the Dry Tortugas. As we were to discover, other boats in the anchorage were small fishing boats, anxious to trade lobster or shrimp for a bottle of liquor or some packs of cigarettes. These were about forty feet long, had wash clothing hanging on the life-lines, and chickens aboard. I wasn't sure where they were from, but had a suspicion they were from Cuba.

After a couple of nights at the Dry Tortugas, *Bafo* returned to the Key West charter company, no worse for the wear.

The James River:

In the summer of 2006 a sailing friend Lee asked if I wanted to sail with him for a month. He knew that I was recovering from my bout with cancer, which had left me in a weakened state. Lee wasn't sure if he wanted to bring his boat back to the Great Lakes, go to Bermuda or cruise the Chesapeake Bay area. "Bring your passport in case we sail to Bermuda," instructed Lee. Lee was a single-handed sailor having sailed alone back from Bermuda.

His boat was a hybrid about thirty-two feet (not counting the bow-sprit) named *Renegade. Renegade* was a schooner (two masts) with a traditional rigging docked at a Virginia marina on the Rappahannock River near the Chesapeake Bay. I was curious to know where Lee intended to sail, but I think even Lee didn't know. Just in case, before going to Virginia, I figured the distance to Lake Erie via the Hudson River and New York Barge Canal and the distance to Bermuda. I wasn't in condition to be of much help with sail handling or anchoring, at least I could assist with navigation.

Eventually we began to cruise the lower Chesapeake Bay area, sometimes anchoring and sometimes pulling into a marina to eat a decent meal and replenish our supply of ice. Eventually we made our way to Hampton Roads and up the James River to a Newport News marina and an elderly live aboard friend of Lee. We spent a little time experiencing the Mariner's Museum and managed to get a ride with another local live aboard to the historic Jamestown. Lee decided we should sail up the James River to Jamestown and view the historic landing from an anchored position.

As we proceeded up the James River we passed an anchorage of several what appeared to be naval supply ships anchored and tethered together. When we reached the Jamestown area, we anchored across from Jamestown on a bend in the James River. We were surrounded on three sides by

Naval mothballed ships

James River

woodland, which is the Chippokes Plantation State Park. The holding ground was good and we slept well that evening.

Aircraft carriers at Norfolk, VA

The following day we returned to the marina for an evening and to bid farewell to Lee's friend Harry. We again passed the Norfolk Naval ship-yard. The yard looked like any shore based industrial complex with the exception of two aircraft carriers partially blocking the view of shore.

As we were beginning to again enter Chesapeake Bay a naval announcer came on the radio warning of a navel vessel departing and to keep clear. Shortly there after we saw the vessel. It was a nuclear submarine. A small naval speedboat was zig-zagging in front of the submarine obviously for security reasons. Quite a thrilling site to see. We headed northeast to the east shore of what is called the Delmarva Peninsula.

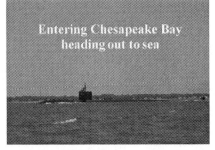
Entering Chesapeake Bay heading out to sea

Descriptions of various anchorages could go on and on. All anchorages seem to have their own particularly memorable aspects as can be noted from the sampling above. The one feature they all seem to have in common is giving one a sense of independence and detachment.

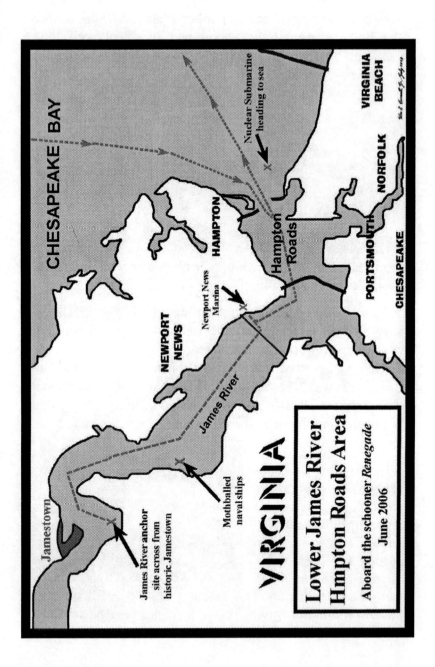

CHESAPEAKE BAY

Nuclear Submarine heading to sea

VIRGINIA BEACH

NORFOLK

HAMPTON

Hampton Roads

PORTSMOUTH

CHESAPEAKE

Newport News Marina

NEWPORT NEWS

James River

VIRGINIA

Lower James River
Hmpton Roads Area

Aboard the schooner *Renegade*
June 2006

Jamestown

James River anchor site across from historic Jamestown

Mothballed naval ships

Epilogue

Before the advent of modern materials wooden sailboats required an inordinate amount of maintenance. Seams had to be caulked, hemp lines often had to be replaced, cotton sails had to be dried before storing and often replaced, wood had to be repaired due to dry-rot. Maintenance often required the work of a full time worker. In short, to own a sailboat or any boat of sufficient size for pleasure, one had be retired or have a substantially above average income. Despite the multitude of improvements resulting in the ability of the not so much higher income individuals, to own a yacht, the stigma of owning a yacht requiring one to be rich has remained to this day.

One of the most interesting aspects of yachting is that nothing stays the same both short and long term. Equipment changes; charts change; materials change; safety devices change; weather changes; rules change; even the water changes. When I studied celestial navigation, it was necessary to determine an accurate time, to the second, from radio signals. Timepieces had to be coordinated with government radio signals emanating from Fort Collins, Colorado or Washington, D.C. with a ticking and a voice announcement of the exact time. Presently, I now have the continuous exact time on my wristwatch and the clock hanging in my office.

Major innovations to boats occur with the passing of each generation. I had the advantages of fiberglass, Dacron, nylon, and polyester developed by a previous generation. I watched the evolution of navigation equipment from a simple radio direction finder to the G.P.S. (geographic positioning system); the introduction of safety equipment such as the EPIRB (emergency position indicating radio beacon), and exact time, all due to satellites. If for some reason, such as war or electro magnetic sun-bursts, these satellites would not operate, would the yachtsman who depended solely on them be helpless?

While the more modern equipment adds to the enjoyment and safety of boating I would caution one to be familiar with alternatives such as knowing the amount of fuel burned per hour calculated with the engine hours to determine amount of remaining fuel in addition to or rather than relying on a fuel gauge; knowing how to navigate based on time, speed and distance in the event the G.P.S. may fail; maintaining a continuous lookout in addition to utilizing radar. It should always be remembered that mechanical and electronic devices are subject to failure.

Finally, to thoroughly enjoy the pleasures of yachting, learning is a continual experience. "CHAPMAN PILOTING SEAMANSHIP & SMALL BOAT HANDLING" is a prerequisite for any boating enthusiast. Numerous free courses are provided by the U.S. Coast Guard and the United States Power Squadron. A cursory perusal of the "Chapman" would indicate that learning about the ways of seamanship and small boat handling is a never-ending experience. The person that purports to know all about seamanship and small boat handling certainly knows little about the sea.

Health and age have forced me to retire and take up a less strenuous activity such as writing this compendium. It is pleasing to know that *Mistress,* now under the caring hands of a daughter and son-in-law, continues the voyage, but now in the Chesapeake Bay area and who knows what waters beyond. May she serve them as well as she served me.

The majesty of a Lake Erie sunset as viewed from Scutters located on the north side of Pelee Island, Ontario.

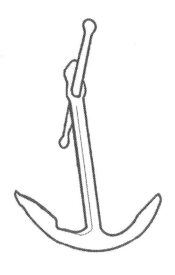